Diane + Scott —
   Here's to a great
2001 and beyond.

        Carol + Don O

The Lack of Money is the Root of all Evil

THE LACK OF ═══ MONEY IS ═══ THE ROOT OF ═══ ALL EVIL ═══

MARK TWAIN'S TIMELESS WISDOM ON MONEY AND WEALTH FOR TODAY'S INVESTOR

ANDREW LECKEY

Prentice Hall Press

Library of Congress Cataloging-in-Publication Data

Leckey, Andrew.
    The lack of money is the root of all evil : Mark Twain's timeless wisdom on money and wealth
    for today's investor / Andrew Leckey.
       p. cm.
    Includes index.
    ISBN 0-7352-0219-2
    1. Investments—United States. 2. Finance, Personal—United States. 3. Money—United States.
    4. Wealth—United States. I. Twain, Mark, 1835-1910. II. Title.
    HG4910.L4433 2001
    332.024—dc21   00-055057
                                                    CIP

Acquisitions Editor: Ellen Schneid Coleman
Production Editor: Mariann Hutlak
Interior Design: Suzanne Behnke
Composition: Robyn Beckerman

This publication is designed to provide accurate and authoritative information in regard to
the subject matter covered. It is sold with the understanding that the publisher is not engaged
in rendering legal, accounting or other professional service. If legal advice or other expert
assistance is required, the services of a competent professional person should be sought.

—From a Declaration of Principles jointly adopted by a Committee of the American Bar
    Association and a Committee of Publishers and Associations.

Printed in the United States of America
10 9 8 7 6 5 4 3 2 1

ISBN 0-7352-0219-2

ATTENTION: CORPORATIONS AND SCHOOLS

Prentice Hall Press books are available at quantity discounts with bulk purchase for edu-
cational, business, or sales promotional use. For information, please write to: Prentice
Hall Special Sales, 240 Frisch Court, Paramus, NJ 07652. Please supply: title of book,
ISBN, quantity, how the book will be used, date needed.

 Paramus, NJ 07652

http://www.phdirect.com

*Dedicated to those who appreciate,
but don't worship, money.*

Ellis & Walery, 54a Baker Street, London, W.

CONTENTS

CONTENTS

ACKNOWLEDGMENTS

I have been fascinated with Mark Twain since reading his books as a youngster, learned more about him while a graduate student at the University of Missouri, and over the years have included some of his quotes in my investment columns. Thanks to my editor, Ellen Schneid Coleman, for encouraging me to take my interest a step further through a book that places Twain's thoughts in a contemporary investment setting. Thanks as well for the assistance of Robert Hirst and Victor Fischer of the Mark Twain Papers at Bancroft Library at the University of California at Berkeley, and for the advice of the investment professionals I consulted in the writing of the book.

FOREWORD

A PROFITABLE LESSON

Mark Twain was more than the greatest humorist of his day. His words still resonate with us, not so much for their timeless wit as for their extraordinary wisdom. His pungent jibs at the way we all live, even today give us a profitable lesson in awareness of who we really and truly *are,* as well as a wonderful sense of self-deprecation that can shake some of our ego out of us and make us wary of our belief that we know all the answers.

Nowhere are Twain's lessons in human frailty more useful than in the financial markets. For, truth told, we have no ability to make the *productive economics* of long-term investing any better. It is already quite good enough. But a solid sense of self-awareness can help us to minimize the *counterproductive emotions* that drive us to a short-term investment focus that defeats our attempt to achieve our long-term goals for wealth accumulation.

So it seems entirely logical, almost inspired, that Andrew Leckey has determined to link Twain's wit and wisdom with Leckey's own common sense perspective on building a successful investment program. A perspective is more important than ever in these days when stock market velocity is so high and financial legerdemain so rife. It's too bad Mark Twain isn't here to comment on what a circus investing has become in recent years. If Twain *were* here today, he might have written something like this:

> Certainly there's no nobler field for human effort than managing other people's money. The more I manage the more I make! And my customer won't have to ask me where my yacht is. As long as I make more for myself than I do for them, my life seems somehow more precious. There is a charm about getting rich—and yachting—which is unspeakable.

These words are not his, of course, but they happen to be necessary to bring Mark Twain's wisdom into contemporary investing. Consider these two examples:

◆ "October. This is one of the peculiarly dangerous months to speculate in stocks. The others are July, January, September, April, November, May, March, June, December, August, and February." Not only was Twain making a timeless point —that *all* months are dangerous for speculation —but in an eerily accurate prophesy. For he began the list with *October,* the month of two of America's greatest stock market crashes: Black Thursday (October 24, 1929) and Black Monday (October 19, 1987).

◆ "... the fool saith, 'put not all thy eggs in the one basket;' but the wise man saith, 'put all your eggs in one basket and watch that basket.'" In today's financial markets, both fool and wise man can follow the same strategy: Own the stocks of all the corporate "eggs" in America, and hold them forever. But even though you've thus achieved complete diversification, watch carefully to make sure that the single all-stock-market basket is administered at minuscule cost.

◆ "It is strange the way the ignorant and inexperienced so often and undeservedly succeed, when the informed and experienced fail." This quotation is stunningly close to Warren Buffet's famous words, 'By periodically investing in an index fund, the know-nothing investor can actually out-perform most investment professionals. Paradoxically, when "dumb" money acknowledges its limitations, it ceases to be dumb.' Buffet, of course, is talking about the certainty that simply owing the stock market basket will provide nearly 100% of the market's return, while—simply because of cost—the average manager will provide about 75% to 80% of that return.

Mutual fund sales charges, advisory fees, and operating expenses can, in Leckey's words, "hoodwink" you. In one of the book's strongest chapters (Chapter 47), he urges you to carefully examine how much you pay for your funds. As his book points out, the secret of successful investing lies mostly in common sense—diversify, keep costs low, minimize portfolio turnover, invest regularly, don't fool with market timing, and above all, invest for the long haul. Again and again, using Mark Twain's wit and wisdom, Andrew Leckey drums these vital lessons home. If you learn them well and follow them faithfully, you will, inevitably in my view, be rewarded with capital accumulations that nicely surpass those of your neighbors.

In his tour of Twain's insights, Leckey gives us all of the appropriate warnings—about speculation (be careful), financial bubbles (they burst), investment newsletters (their "prophesy-guns" often misfire), and shareholder's rights (you *do* need "a new deal"). When all is said and done, Mark Twain said,

"Make money and the whole world will conspire to call you a gentleman." Following the wisdom and common sense contained in this volume will help you earn the money you need for a comfortable future, and "gentleman"—or "lady"—you will be called. Get used to it!

John C. Bogle

PREFACE

Investing in Mark Twain

No matter what the markets do in the long or short run, Mark Twain is a growth stock, a surer thing than any inside tip on the Kentucky Derby. His celebrity as a personality roars ahead with *Adventures of Huckleberry Finn* for an after-burner. The argument about whether high schools should make it required reading saves it from falling into Twain's category of "Classic: A book which people praise and don't read." Though so many scholar-critics keep discussing his career and writings that he might rate as a smokestack industry, he is essentially high-tech. Check out websites such as york.ca/twainweb or marktwain.miningco.com. Ask for help on the Mark Twain Forum *TWAIN-L@YORKU.CA* or get on the e-mail loop at *marktwain.guide@about.com.* Through *ebay.com* you can bid for not just first editions of his books, but for memorabilia and for near-junk that you never suspected of being *the universe,* as he once put it.

Impatient enough to tear all the buttons off a starched shirt or to push a bulky umbrella inside out, Twain would have menaced an unforgiving, light-touch keyboard. But, fascination would have kept him contending with the latest software or hand-sized gizmos; he would have clipped pagers doubt-lessly to his butler, probably to his daughters, and maybe to his cats. Proof comes from his being so quick to try out the type-writer, telephone, Dictaphone, and the tricky, high-front-wheel bicycle—for a few years, the acme of personalized speed. Photographs show him cruising trustfully in the earliest practi-cal automobiles.

Any talk about Twain and inventions leads inescapably to that mechanical typesetter that recycled two hundred thousand of his nineteenth-century dollars. Too many biographers devalue him as a reckless speculator or even a clueless gambler, the breed that subsidizes those lavish casinos in Las Vegas: the plunger, who deep-down believes that Luck/Fortune is on his or her side no matter how long he or she builds the suspense, or else keeps doubling up because the "laws" of probability are sure to kick in. Still, while Twain knew and talked much about gam-bling (at cards, not dice), and—a good sign—often joked about it, there's no proof that he lost heavily, much less compulsively. As investor, Twain went not for "corners" in pork-bellies, but for inventions, productive machines or processes. While admittedly hoping to earn millions, he aimed to help improve technology and, therefore, humankind's prosperity, intellectual as well as material. That mechanical typesetter would speed up the circu-lation of the printed word which made enlightenment wider, deeper, and cheaper than ever before.

But hot-lead type has sunk into the Sargasso Sea of obso-lescence. Today Twain is an energy stock mergable with any hot-button enterprise. Tom Sawyer or Huck Finn would have boggled at Mark Twain as *educator* or, less derisively, as *family man.* But they would take an option on Twain as *tourist* or—

still ahead—as *sports fan* (baseball, anyway). 'Energy is Eternal Delight,' argued William Blake. Characteristically, Twain would pick up on the news about radium and would have fun with it rather than feel threatened. His mind and temperament kept radiating in many directions. Until old age (and, arguably, most days even then) he felt that he could never get around to everything worth knowing, doing, or saying. As an investor now, he would still be a bull. But a socially responsible one, not like Jay Gould, whom he detested so much that the shape-shifting shark-bear-shark never got a chance to tell him he was among Gould's three favorite authors.

When pushed past the generalities, Twain as investor gets complicated, and so do the people who estimate that side of him. He talked disproportionately more about his losses—his mistakes instead of his smart moves which were fewer, to be sure. Blunders do pay better dividends in humor; pratfalls will amuse humankind until it grows dullingly noble. No matter how heartily serious the crowd cheers for a strutting winner, it will chuckle if he slips on a rolled up copy of the *The Wall Street Journal*. Even Twain's devotees will rate him as a gullible, ineducable failure at handling money. They may find relief for having played too safe themselves or they may prefer to get their warnings against risk posed entertainingly. The conflicting possibilities keep Twain the businessman as alive today as his other personas. A few admirers, still inclined to believe that prosperity is the mark (no pun!) God sets on virtue, choose to focus on his luxurious houses, luxuriously run, in Hartford and Redding, Connecticut. Others, who easily catch what the Germans mean by *Schadenfreude,* choose to feature his failures and not to compute how much he earned during his lifetime or, more narrowly, how effectively he bargained over the prices for his writings. They keep improving on his yarn about how he refused to plug into Alexander Graham Bell's financing. The most balanced or balancing admirers enjoy his ups and downs—making it big. Losing still bigger, making it back again bigger still.

Eventually, whatever the theorizing, we had better settle down to facts and common-sense decisions, as Twain always did. He never turned so fanciful as to bring his soup spoon up to his ear. A fellow-humorist decided that Twain was like the clown taking up tickets at the circus: He amuses, but he means business. In a *Burlesque Book of Etiquette* that Twain never finished, he advised for "At the Don-Fight": "Let your secret sympathies and your compassion be always with the underdog—this is magnanimity; but, bet on the other one—this is business." Since Andrew Leckey turns Twain's wit to practical use admirably, I will merely doodle around the edges.

First, if you value Twain's sayings watch out for knock-offs. Retailers, that is, retellers wanting a bigger clientele put his name on somebody else's words. "Everybody talks about the weather, but nobody does anything about it." Or, in honest reverence, they sign his proxy under a witticism they think worthy of him. "There are three kinds of lies: lies, damned lies, and statistics." Or immodestly helping out genius, they manufacture a maxim that he should have thought up. "The art of prophecy is very difficult, especially with respect to the future."

Second, Twain did drop into (corporate) bankruptcy, a few years after he exulted to a crony, "Whatever I touch turns to gold." He learned that over-confidence can sink harder than a lead balloon; he never joked about going to court guided by attorneys and accountants. *Verbum sap* (though Twain did not pun habitually).

Third, while Twain died wealthy, he had learned by then to navigate Wall Street knowledgeably. In fact, the in-depth record of his last hurrah might look to the (later) SEC like insider trading. He did consort with many of the leading millionaires besides Andrew Carnegie. Both Thomas Fortune Ryan and August Belmont II turned out for the dinner on his sixty-seventh birthday. The next year, at a pre-sailing dinner for him within the pricey Metropolitan Club, over half of the twenty guests were identifiable in *Who's Who in America, 1903-1905* as industrialists, financiers, or plain "capitalists." Leckey presents Henry Huttleston Rogers as Twain's "financial advisor." That's a brave understatement either for how Rogers operated with and for Standard Oil or for how he handled Twain's accounts for almost fifteen years and shaped an estate still worth tender, loving care from the Chase Manhattan Bank.

Finally, Twain as investor adds up to the same best advice as from his other selves: Keep mentally flexible and alert and hold on to your sense of humor because sooner or later you will need it, not only to write your own "Burlesque Book of Etiquette." Twain's book includes: "If you live in the country, buy at 80, sell at 40. Avoid all forms of eccentricity."

As for serious rules on investing, Twain would settle, I think, for the Fourteen (Wilsonian) Points at the end of Leckey's Introduction.

Louis J. Budd

INTRODUCTION
A TWAIN FOR TODAY

Mark Twain understood money as well as he understood human nature. We can learn from his humor, his admonitions, and his mistakes. His basic advice—to employ common sense in investment choices, while setting aside some ammunition for speculation—is well-suited to a twenty-first century in which blue-chip and high-tech investing exist side by side. Like many celebrities, he ran into credit problems and required the help of a shrewd financial planner to get his finances back into shape.

One of the most famous and frequently-quoted American writers, the humorist and novelist Mark Twain was born Samuel Langhorne Clemens in poverty in Missouri in 1835 and died a wealthy man in Connecticut in 1910. Money, or the lack of money, was a strong component in his observations about the human condition. In expanding their portfolios, modern investors scrutinize initial public offerings and the volatile stocks tied to the Internet, just as investors in Twain's time scouted the possibilities of precious metals and stocks of newfangled inventions such as the telephone. He lived in an "anything goes" world—not unlike today's—full of financial volatility, scurrilous scams, and headline-grabbing wealthy industrialists. Amid this din, he never took himself too seriously. "Ah, well, I am a great and sublime fool," Twain once penned in a letter, putting himself in his place. "But then I am God's fool, and all his works must be contemplated with respect."

Writing for readers of all ages, Twain left an immense legacy. It's little wonder that his witty, never-dull personal letters now command $1,000 a page at auction. Regarding the work ethic, for example, Twain wrote the famous tale of Tom Sawyer sweet-talking his friends into paying him with an apple, marbles, firecrackers, and other prized possessions for the privilege of whitewashing Aunt Polly's fence in *The Adventures of Tom Sawyer*. Twain loved a good wager, and early in his writing career was told a funny story about a frog-jumping bet that was lost when someone fed buckshot to one of the top leapers in order to weigh it down. The short story "The Celebrated Jumping Frog of Calaveras County" that he wrote for an eastern magazine catapulted him to immediate and lasting national fame. His first novel *The Gilded Age: A Tale of To-day* lampooned big business "fat cats" and America's obsession with getting rich; its title became the name for that wealth-absorbed era. His other novels such as *Adventures of Huckleberry Finn*, assorted short stories, speeches, and personal letters were part of his lifelong battle against small-mindedness, injustice, and cruelty. As another great American novelist, Ernest Hemingway, pointed out: "All modern American literature comes from one book by Mark Twain called *Huckleberry Finn*."

A devotee of technological innovation and the stock market, Twain, were he still alive today, would likely be trading online, scouring for IPOs, and cursing under his breath any telecom stocks that weren't living up to his lofty expectations. Since he often sold his books himself by subscription rather than going through conventional publishers, it's not hard to envision him constructing his own web site to do the very same. His approach to investment, work, and meeting financial demands remains relevant. Were he still around, he might be providing uproarious commentary as to what on earth Microsoft billionaire Bill Gates could possibly be doing with all of his wealth, or estimating how many buildings really required real estate magnate Donald Trump's name on them. He could be commending unassuming billionaire Warren Buffett of Berkshire Hathaway for his ability to keep both financial gains and losses in perspective. He may have forged friendships with common-sense investment leaders such as low-cost mutual fund proponent Jack Bogle of Vanguard Group or "buy-what-you-really-like" stock-picker Peter Lynch of Fidelity Investments. Twain never forgot the past, but was energized by the prospects in both the present and future. What would he make of Cisco Systems Inc. mushrooming in a quick 14 years to become the most valuable company on earth in 2000, boasting a market value of more than $555 billion? Big technology has become the equivalent of the big railroads and big oil of his time.

"Been there, done that" could have been Twain's motto. He amassed great wealth by age 50, his publishing company went bankrupt when he was 60, and he became wealthy again at 70, avoiding personal bankruptcy and eventually leaving an estate valued at nearly half a million dollars after his death. A wealthy oil executive helped him tie together lucrative copyright agreements that would greatly benefit Twain's descendants. He lived in a time when there were few financial safety nets provided by the government and a panic could quickly wipe out a fortune. Despite leaving school at age twelve upon his father's death, as an adult he was awarded honorary degrees from Yale University, the University of Missouri, and Oxford University. A stubborn "Missouri mule" mindset served to pull Twain through all his circumstances. While he did not worship money, he always found that having it around was immeasurably helpful. As the first famous American to write in his country's common tongue, he was clear-headed and viciously funny in presenting timeless observations on the vicissitudes of the investment world and man's misadventures in attempting to cope with them. In a letter, Twain wrote:

> "I have worked there at all the different trades and professions known to the catalogues. I have been everything from a newspaper editor down to a cow-catcher on a locomotive, and I am encouraged to believe that if there had been a few more occupations to experiment on I might have made a dazzling success at last and found out what mysterious designs Providence had in creating me."

He prospected for silver and gold in Nevada and California, was a riverboat pilot on the Mississippi, and worked as a printer in New York and Philadelphia. His other occupations included newspaper editor and reporter, travel writer, and world-class lecturer. Twain took out patents on numerous inventions. These included a highly successful self-pasting scrapbook, an automatic typesetting machine that was too delicate to be practical, and a nutritional supplement that never caught on. He was relentlessly working up ideas for inventions to the very end of his life. "Sometimes he so liked the idea of making big money that he neglected his own talent," Robert Hirst, general editor of the Mark Twain Papers told me during a visit to that office at the

Bancroft Library of the University of California at Berkeley. "And to him an inventor was next to God." A forward thinker, Twain claimed to have been the first American to have a telephone in his private residence and also the first person to apply the typewriter to literature, when he wrote *Tom Sawyer*. Modern inventions such as television and atomic energy appeared in his works. "It was a stunning little century, for sure, that nineteenth!" Twain wrote in an essay. "But it's a poor thing compared to what the twentieth is going to be."

From his riverboat experience, he adopted his pen-name Mark Twain, a boatman's cry that signified a water depth of two fathoms, or twelve feet, a downright worrisome level for a steamboat. As an avid buyer and seller of stock, he loved to poke fun at the irresistible urge to speculate and at his own pratfalls in trying to do so. For example, he fell prey to speculative mining stocks and failed to buy early Bell Telephone stock offered to him for a give-away price. He was fascinated by scoundrels seeking to snatch the money of others, two prime examples being the shameless King and Duke con men in *Huckleberry Finn,* who misrepresented themselves before an entire community before they were eventually tarred, feathered, and ridden out of town on a rail. Get-rich-quick schemes such as the phony gold mines of his day correlate to today's "cold" telephone sales calls and over-hyped Internet pitches. All that glitters still is not gold.

Splendid in his stylish, year-round white suit a century before modern novelist Tom Wolfe assumed that calculated look, Twain became America's first celebrity and continued to hold that title for many decades. He once referred to himself as "the most conspicuous person on the planet" and was indeed a citizen of the world. Even today, his caricature with flowing white hair and full mustache can be mistaken for no other individual. A great communicator, his around-the-world lecture tours made him rich because everyone loved his wit and wisdom. He made nearly a thousand one-night lecture stops in endless small towns and kibitzed with high society in major cities around the globe. Twain's comments offer the same spark today as they did in his time, and continue to merit repeating. Besides noting the common traits of men, he poked fun at the hype surrounding the richest industrialists of the time, men such as Commodore Cornelius Vanderbilt, whom he considered lacking in human kindness. His words had serious impact. For example, Twain's humorous comments on the crass unfairness of a corporate board that included the phrase "new deal" led to President Franklin D. Roosevelt coining the name for his famous economic plan to pull America out of the Great Depression.

"I am the whole human race without a detail lacking; I have studied the human race with diligence and strong interest all these years in my own person, in myself," said Twain, who "walked the walk" of many lifestyles. "I find in big or little proportion every quality and every defect that is findable in the mass of the race." He immortalized the poor folk in his hometown of Hannibal, Missouri, in his writings, yet also wrote of the stuffy nature of the royal class he met in England, where his books were best sellers. A friend of President Ulysses S. Grant, Twain arranged publication of Grant's *Personal Memoirs,* which garnered for Grant's widow the largest royalty check ever written at that time. He dined with the likes of Kaiser Wilhelm II and the Prince of Wales. Shortly before Twain's death, he played miniature golf with President Woodrow Wilson in

Bermuda. Yet despite such hobnobbing, his works never lost touch with the average man, woman, and child, eloquently presenting their basic goodness, foibles, and human shortcomings.

This book is built upon humorous, cynical, insightful, and outrageous sayings about investment and money management from famous Twain novels such as *Adventures of Huckleberry Finn, The Adventures of Tom Sawyer, A Connecticut Yankee in King Arthur's Court, The Innocents Abroad, The Gilded Age, Pudd'nhead Wilson,* and *Roughing It,* as well as Twain's many short stories, speeches, personal letters, and published letters to editors. In each case, a tie-in to circumstances affecting today's investor is a primary objective. Money and human nature are two concepts that have not changed fundamentally since Twain's time.

Were this pundit of the nineteenth and early twentieth centuries still around to formulate a "common-sense" investment guide for the citizens of the twenty-first century, it might conceivably include points such as these:

1. Don't take financial tips from know-nothings or crooks.
2. Whenever you fall, always get up again, and do so with honor.
3. Have plenty of stable investments, but also embrace technology. It is, after all, the future.
4. Beware of scams. They don't change much over the years; only the victims are new.
5. Being broke has little to recommend it—ever.
6. When taking risks, keeping in mind that speculation could also be the death of you.

7. Be wary of easy credit. Its terms are not easy.

8. Understand that saving requires painful discipline. (Especially painful for you.)

9. Hunting for fortune can sometimes be just as gratifying as actually finding it.

10. Never be cowed by the wealth of others. What makes you think they're any better than you?

11. Know the value of a dollar, ponder it, and hold onto that dollar tightly.

12. Never forget your financial roots. In fact, you could wind up back there again someday.

13. Accept that some folks will always think their money is somehow better than yours. Let them worry about that, not you.

14. Realize that, no matter how much money you acquire, you still can't take it with you.

One gentle word of caution: The words of Twain were not designed for "stick-in-the-muds." He was to the very end a billiard-playing, cigar-chomping, youthful thinker blessed with a very pointed and sometimes brutal sarcasm. Therefore, a sense of humor about both money and yourself is required for this book. Otherwise, you really won't enjoy your gains from smart investing and money handling anyway. So relax and ease into the Twain spirit. "I like a good story well told," he once said in a speech. "That is the reason I am sometimes forced to tell them myself."

The Lack of
≡ Money is ≡
the Root of
≡ all Evil ≡

1

NO TIME IS REALLY
THE WORST OR BEST
TIME TO INVEST

> "October. This is one of the peculiarly dangerous months to speculate in stocks in. The others are July, January, September, April, November, May, March, June, December, August and February."
>
> *(Pudd'nhead Wilson)*

Though just one of many worrisome months to Mark Twain's way of thinking, October continues to be the cruelest month for the stock market. The infamous crashes of 1929 and 1987 both occurred in October, and that month has produced some truly harrowing experiences in subsequent years as well. These sudden collapses in the value of stocks that sent the market averages into a tailspin were kicked off by high stock prices and inadequate trading controls, the same ingredients that triggered market panics during Twain's time. Fearful investors rush to unload their stock, making the situation worse as stocks fall lower and lower in value.

The 1987 decline was made even more intense by computerized program trading, in which computers programmed to buy and sell large quantities of stock were triggered automatically when prices hit predetermined levels. That's not quite like the old "smoke-filled room" of Twain's day, when brokerage executives would gather to carefully decide which stocks had done well for the company and might conceivably be worth keeping. The computer exhibits no loyalty or emotional tug to slow its quick dumping of equities deemed unworthy. After 1987, market safeguards called *circuit breakers* were put into place to slow or halt trading when the markets have declined too far or too quickly, though the jury is still out on their real effectiveness.

Twain's quote is from "Pudd'nhead Wilson's Calendar," a whimsical almanac written by the fictional small-town attorney David Wilson, the title character of the novel *Pudd'nhead Wilson*. As this entry points out, trying to invest at the bottom of a slow market or pick the top of a hot market in any given month is a foolish game of chance. Twain himself experienced his greatest problems when he tried to speculate in mining stocks and other risky ventures, either overextending himself or getting in at precisely the wrong time. These days there are investment letters and pundits that do nothing else but try to time the market. Even the experts regularly botch this exercise, so average investors should forget about it altogether. Furthermore, no market cycle exactly duplicates any previous one in history, making precedence a risky indicator. For example, early in the year is traditionally a strong period for small-company stocks and certain industries do have periods of the year when they tend to excel, yet all months can be "peculiarly dangerous."

Twenty-first century Americans appear to be fearless, investing far more of their money in stocks than ever before in history. They're also willing to invest in stocks that carry much greater risk, adjusting to their constant volatility. The average active investor, as measured by the American Association of Individual Investors, has increased stocks to 75 percent of his or her portfolio, up from 60 percent in 1994. Nearly half of all American households now own stock, up from just 12 percent in 1975. Over half of the stock of the nation's 1,000 largest companies is now owned by individuals rather than by institutional investors such as pension funds, according to the Conference Board. Average investors are also leading the charge to volatile technology stocks, with individuals and company officials owning more than half of America Online, Dell Computer, Bell Atlantic, AT&T, and Microsoft Corp. Individuals have a much smaller stake in companies such as Citigroup, Home Depot, and Bristol-Myers Squibb. Even the conservative National Association of Investors Corp., which sponsors investment clubs, now has nearly half of its NAIC Top 100 in tech stocks. Furthermore, the average stock fund now has nearly one-third of its portfolio in technology, according to Morningstar Inc.

While an average investor should carefully buy stocks for the long haul and forget about market timing, certain aspects of market performance should be understood:

◆ The stock market will always have recurring cycles, with bull markets moving upward before the market drops 20 percent and becomes a growling bear market. Neither the bull nor the bear stays with us forever.

◆ Upward movement in the market tends to be more gradual, while a reversal can occur quite precipitously, giving investors quite a shock to their systems. Sometimes a market trend can last years, while in today's computerized world that exaggerates trends it can come and go within mere days or weeks.

◆ Ample money supply, low interest rates, strong employment, and political and economic stability are definite pluses for the market.

◆ Tight money, tax increases, high interest rates, high unemployment, international surprises, and upcoming elections can be a drag on its progress.

All these carefully analyzed trends simply provide a helpful backdrop worth considering, not anything absolute to which one should religiously adhere. The fact that stock trading goes on nearly 24 hours a day, on dozens of different exchanges around the world, can continue or accelerate any trend that began in any one market. Be on guard, but not paranoid. Twain was more than willing to take chances with investments, but his overall philosophy was grounded in reality. He knew exactly what he was doing. Using one's common sense also makes outstanding sense today.

2

KEEP TABS ON
YOUR MONEY—AND
EVERYTHING ELSE

> "Behold, the fool saith, 'Put not all thine eggs in the
> one basket'—which is but a manner of saying,
> 'Scatter your money and your attention;' but the wise
> man saith, 'Put all your eggs in one basket and—
> WATCH THAT BASKET.'"
>
> *(Pudd'nhead Wilson)*

A tale of switched identities at birth and the dire repercussions that followed, *Pudd'nhead Wilson* underscores the importance of keeping track of everything. The fact that many investors fail to watch their financial baskets altogether is today a greater concern than in Mark Twain's time because there are so many different sorts of investments available. Investors toss money into mutual funds, stocks, bonds, annuities, or insurance policies, spurred by glowing articles in the financial press or by the demands of tax-related transactions. They stash the necessary paperwork in a drawer or safe deposit box, then forget about the holdings altogether except for paying tax on them. Investment company statements go unopened and are ultimately thrown away.

Surprisingly, this happens to individuals at all levels of the income scale. Because they can't be bothered to keep track, these folks may wind up subsequently investing in other vehicles that are virtually the same as the ones they already own. Not only do they forget what they have; they fail to keep other family members apprised of their holdings. Major trends in investing pass them by or their portfolios are quietly eaten up by annual expenses or fees. Sometimes a portfolio will include the stock of bankrupt companies or firms that no longer fulfill the role they did decades earlier.

Another mistake that investors typically make when they "scatter" their money and attention is to buy so many different sorts of investments for the sake of diversification that there's no way anyone can intelligently track them. It is common to buy funds or stocks on every possible "top 10" list that is published, resulting in a hodgepodge of holdings instead of a coordinated portfolio designed to meet goals. Some of the holdings may actually counteract each other. Diversification should be a thought-out process that begins with building up a cash cushion to protect against emergencies, emphasizing money-market funds or bank certificates of deposit.

Here are some tips on formulating an effective savings and investment game plan:

◆ Having money automatically deducted from your paycheck is a good idea for building your nest egg at a bank, mutual fund company, or brokerage firm. Such enforced saving is hardly noticed.

✦ Expand from saving into investing by putting money in several low-minimum-requirement stock mutual funds. Initially select broad-based "core" holdings rather than highly specialized funds that could be more volatile.

✦ After you've built some profits in mutual funds, the next step could be individual stocks. Begin there with some well-known blue-chip stocks that should provide a reliable foundation for your portfolio. Depending on your tax situation, you might buy tax-exempt mutual bonds, too.

Always be sure to take advantage of your company's 401(k) retirement plan, individual retirement accounts (IRAs), or Keogh plans for the self-employed. By emphasizing a small, diversified group of investments in which you have confidence, you can remain firmly in control of your personal wealth. Pick what works best with your own tolerance toward risk. Don't hide your money under the mattress, but do select investments that let you sleep at night and that can be monitored regularly.

A BUSINESS TRIP

The Adventures of Tom Sawyer

3
BEHOLD THE
LIFESTYLES OF THE
RICH AND FAMOUS

"The low level which commercial morality has reached in America is deplorable. We have humble God fearing Christian men among us who will stoop to do things for a million dollars that they ought not to be willing to do for less than 2 million."

The number of zeroes behind the dollar sign has increased since Mark Twain complained about overpaid industrialists, yet society is still scratching its head over the compensation of some of the mortals who walk among us. For example, Computer Associates chief executive officer Charles Wang drew total compensation of $650 million in fiscal year 1999, while America Online CEO Stephen Case brought home $117 million. When homerun hitter Ken Griffey Jr. signed a $116.5 million, nine-year contract with the Cincinnati Reds in February 2000, professional baseball commissioner Bud Selig greeted the signing by shouting,

"Thank you! Thank you very much!" Griffey had accepted about half his market value just so he could play in his hometown and have his dad as one of the coaches.

Getting by on $12.5 million a year will be a challenge, but at least Griffey is a winner. From 1994 through 1998, Fruit of the Loom chief executive William Farley was paid $60.6 million, including salary, bonus, and options, even though his company lost $247 million and ultimately filed for Chapter 11 bankruptcy protection. Meanwhile, people continue to be astounded by the more than $100 billion in net worth that today keeps Microsoft's Bill Gates in the top spot as richest man in the United States. As the late Sen. Everett McKinley Dirksen of Illinois once observed on government budgets: "A billion here, a billion there, pretty soon you're talkin' real money!"

Television quiz shows glorify becoming a millionaire by using one's brainpower to answer questions on trivia or historical facts. However, the largest batch of millionaires in recent years has been spawned in quite a different way. The incentive stock option at work has been the ticket for many folks who don't hit homeruns or manage junk bonds. It permits an employee to purchase shares of company stock under conditions that meet Internal Revenue Service criteria. Once strictly for top executives, the incentive stock option is now more generally available to workers at all levels and is frequently used to lure new employees. Salary is no longer the only consideration when taking a job, as it once was. "They're offering me stock options" is the happy outcry at many fast-growing "dot-com" companies.

Here are some important considerations for any employee being offered incentive stock options as part of a compensation package:

+ Find out what other companies are offering at your position level.

+ Determine what percentage of the company your options actually represent.

+ Realize that the number of options you receive is generally negotiable with the employer.

+ Find out the company's schedule for vesting, which is when rights can pass to you independent of your employment.

+ Ask whether you can continue to vest after you've left the company.

Of course, the quality and growth potential of the specific company can go a long way in determining whether those stock options are likely to be hits or misses. There's a lot more to consider when choosing an employer and there are no assurances of becoming a millionaire. Nonetheless, the fast-paced modern job market dictates that many workers in the hottest fields no longer have to "stoop," as Twain so sarcastically put it, for less than they think they are worth.

HE GAVE HIM TEN CENTS.

Adventures of Huckleberry Finn

4
SPECULATION CAN ROUGH YOU UP

"The bubble scarcely left a microscopic moisture behind it. I was an early beggar and a thorough one. My hoarded stocks were not worth the paper they were printed on. I threw them all away. I, the cheerful idiot that had been squandering money like water, and thought myself beyond the reach of misfortune, had not now as much as fifty dollars when I gathered my various debts and paid them. I removed from the hotel to a very private boarding house."

(Roughing It)

A financial bubble can still pop right in your face. In Mark Twain's case, it involved highly speculative, much-hyped mining stocks that encouragingly shot up in price before plummeting to earth. The mining companies simply didn't produce the precious metals to back up their inflated stock value. *Roughing It,* Twain's second major book, takes place in the aftermath of the California Gold Rush and recounts his early financial misadventures that included a bad case of "silver fever."

The gold and silver booms in California and Nevada that led to Twain's part-time prospecting have similarities to today's frenetic investment in Internet-related stocks and initial public offerings of new companies. "Tech fever" is rampant and the concept of a well-rounded portfolio often goes right out the window. Despite good intentions and logical reasons for investing, not everything will pan out. Twain believed it was fine to take a flyer on a risky investment that shows promise, but one should never plan an entire lifestyle around it. That lifestyle could head south rather suddenly.

Besides authentic investments that don't deliver as promised, there are outright scams, just as in the "good old days" of phony gold mines, faked certificates, claim-robbing, and deeds to nonexistent property. "All through my life I have been the easy prey of the cheap adventurer," Twain wrote in his autobiography. "He came, he lied, he robbed and went his way, and the next one arrived by the next train and began to scrape up what was left."

Today, the rush of do-it-yourself online investors has prompted an avalanche of hype and fraudulent schemes from some crooked online entrepreneurs who see the potential. These can quickly transform self-satisfied grins into frowns, and an opulent lifestyle into threadbare poverty. As in days gone by, many modern scams tout the smallest of "penny" stocks and offer a pitch that promises everything but the moon. The Internet has become the primary tool for misleading newsletters, bulletin boards, and advertisements. Crooks feel that the rush of novice investors to the Internet and to online trading provides a steady stream of potential patsies. Their practices also damage the credibility of reputable firms promoting products and investments online.

High-tech crooks are cheeky these days. One fledgling telecom company, for example, retracted its posted claim that it would have $1 billion in sales within four years only after the Securities and Exchange Commission insisted that it do so. Nonetheless, the company still paid one stock promoter 75,000 shares to hype its supposed prospects, and millions of dollars worth of shares traded in a couple of days based solely on misleading press releases. Somebody made a lot of money, but it sure wasn't investors. This firm with no profits, employees, or research continued to raise millions by selling bonds and warrants to unsophisticated investors who believed its tall tales.

Lies now travel incredibly fast. Just a few years ago, the only way to distribute information about the smallest over-the-counter stocks that didn't meet stock exchange requirements was through broker cold-calling or direct mail using financial magazine subscriber lists. That required work and start-up money. Not only has the Internet lowered costs for investors, it has made it possible for fraud to be conducted cheaply with far greater outreach. Some fraudulent Internet sites look as professional and slick as reputable ones, with made-up press releases and news reports included. Looks can deceive, for you can't tell a web site by its home page.

Telling lies on the Internet is the same as lying to investors on the telephone. Take the necessary precautions:

♦ Don't assume that any information from newsletters, message boards, or advertisements is true until you've done your homework and can prove it.

✦ Check the investment professional, firm, product, or service in question by calling the appropriate local, state, or federal regulator to determine whether there is proper licensing.

✦ Find out the regulatory records of the parties involved.

✦ Download to your computer and print a hard copy of any online solicitation you're considering.

While there is always risk in investing, you'll be kicking yourself if you don't prepare for that uncertainty. This way, you may avoid a fall that would have you "roughing it" yourself.

5
DIVIDE AND CONQUER YOUR PORTFOLIO

"In my experience, previously counted chickens
never do hatch. How many of mine I have counted!—
& never a one of them but failed! It is much better to
hedge disappointment by not counting. Unexpected
money is a delight. The same sum is a bitterness
when you expected more."

High expectations for the stock market in recent years have resulted in bitter disappointment for some investors who counted their stock and mutual fund profits before they hatched. "Providence always makes a point to find out what you are after, so as to see that you don't get it," Mark Twain once wrote to a friend. The marked differences in the returns of seemingly similar investments are a big reason why asset allocation remains crucial. It involves dividing up holdings among different types of assets, such as domestic stocks, international stocks, bonds, cash, and real estate. As in Twain's day, putting together a sensible formula for your investment portfolio revolves around how soon you may need your money. No one wants to be left a day late and a dollar short.

While stocks and real estate offer splendid long-term returns, they tend to fluctuate in value and should only be chosen if you don't really need the money for a number of years. Bonds and cash, despite lower returns, make more sense for shorter periods of time, especially if you're closing in on retirement or about to pay for a college education. You don't want to experience a big drop in the value of your holdings just before either of those events occurs. Due to withdrawal penalties and taxes, retirement accounts should always be considered long-term money. If there's a chance you might need your money quickly, mutual funds provide easy access. A number of funds, however, charge withdrawal fees during the first several years of ownership. Also keep tax considerations in mind whenever selecting investments, especially in regard to tax-exempt municipal bonds or tax-efficient mutual funds.

There's no one right asset allocation, because you must select one that best fits your investment personality:

♦ *A conservative investor,* for example, might have 40 percent of a portfolio in stocks, 40 percent in bonds, and 20 percent in cash instruments such as money-market funds. This means less volatility and more stability of principle. The selection process may also include investing in large blue-chip companies with proven track records. Older investors typically fit in this category, choosing some bonds for income and stability over the greater growth potential of stocks.

+ *A moderate investor* could have 65 percent in stocks, 25 percent in bonds, and 10 percent in cash. This provides some kick, but doesn't keep anyone from sleeping soundly at night.

+ *An aggressive investor* may prefer 85 percent in stocks, 10 percent in bonds, and 5 percent in cash. Some pundits say young people could even have 100 percent of their investment portfolios in stocks because their time horizon is so long that short term losses mean little. The younger person is also willing to "take a flyer" on some flashy new companies whose prospects are hardly assured.

The trend toward technology stocks has thrown many typical stock measures completely out of whack, but a traditional, common-sense approach to investing still makes sense when considering more traditional companies. It's not a bad idea for tech stocks as well, though many emerging companies don't live up to the historic earnings criteria simply because they don't generate earnings yet. Ultimately, your decisions will be tied not only to what portion of your portfolio you want in the stock market, but how that stock portion will be broken down into industry groups such as technology, health care, financials, and transportation. When you do decide to invest, compare the data for individual companies to others within their industry, rather than with dissimilar types of firms. Otherwise, you're comparing apples to oranges.

Here are some important concepts to understand when making stock choices:

+ *Earnings per share* is the portion of a company's profit allocated to each outstanding share of common stock.

Look for companies that have seen a steady increase over five years.

✦ *Price/earnings ratio* divides the current price of a stock by its earnings per share for the last 12 months. A P/E of 30 means investors are paying 30 times earnings for the stock. Due to the bull market and the technology boom, many P/Es have gone much higher than traditional levels.

✦ *Book value,* or *stockholders' equity,* is the difference between a company's assets and its liabilities.

✦ The *return on equity* measures how much the company earns on the stockholders' equity and is especially helpful when comparing companies within an industry.

✦ The current and projected *dividends* are also worth checking, in particular with an income portfolio. It's smart to watch for companies who are consistent in their dividends and have significant ownership by mutual funds and pension funds.

✦ It's also a positive if a company is likely to *split* its stock, even though it does not actually increase your financial holdings of the stock. Splitting does, however, typically draw attention to the company and often results in a price increase after the split.

✦ *Beta* is a measure of price volatility that shows you how a stock is moving relative to changes in the Standard & Poor's 500 stock index. The S&P 500 has a beta coefficient of 1, so any stock with a higher beta is more volatile than the market, and any with a lower beta is expected to rise and fall more slowly than the market. Conservative investors should emphasize stocks with low betas.

The poker term "blue chip" is used in reference to the biggest, best-known companies that are often included in core investment accounts, the portfolios of more conservative investors, or large pension funds. The 25 most valuable companies as of April 2000 were Cisco Systems (ticker symbol CSCO) at $555 billion, followed, in order, by General Electric (GE); Microsoft (MSFT); Intel (INTC); Exxon Mobil (XOM); Wal-Mart Stores (WMT); Vocafone AirTouch (VOD); Nokia (NOK); International Business Machines (IBM); Oracle (ORCL); Citigroup (C); Lucent Technologies (LU); Toyota Motor (TM); Deutsche Tekekom AG (DT); AT&T; (T); American International Group (AIG); BP Amoco Plc (BPA); Nortel Networks (NT); Sun Microsystems (SUNW); Merck (MRK); SBC Communications (SBC); France Telecom (FTE); Pfizer (PFE); Home Depot (HD); and America Online (AOL).

INNOCENT DREAMS.

Roughing It

6

ANTICIPATE TOMORROW'S TRENDS TODAY

> "About the end of the year (1877) I put up a telephone wire from my house down to the *Courant* (newspaper) office, the only telephone wire in town, and the first one that was ever used in a private house in the world."
>
> *The Autobiography of Mark Twain*

New, newer, newest. In Mark Twain's time, the telephone was the hottest personal technology gadget. He just had to have one, not only because it helped in his work, but because it was new and he always fancied himself a forward thinker. He was similarly fascinated with the workings of precision pocket watches. Meanwhile, science fiction author Jules Verne, Twain's contemporary, wrote of submarines, dirigibles, and space travel, using amazingly accurate hypotheses based on rational scientific detail. Technology was a national fascination then as it is now.

At the beginning of the twentieth century, investment libraries were crammed with shelf after shelf of books pondering the potential of the stocks of that day's most powerful transportation vehicle, the railroad. Scrutiny of railroad pricing and efficiency of trunk lines couldn't, of course, predict the advent of automobiles and airplanes. New industries will always be a calculated bet in an ever-changing field that makes sudden moves when you least expect them. Many technologies and trends appear and disappear regularly. Others don't prove to be as important as had been predicted. As Twain described it: "Civilization: A limitless multiplication of unnecessary necessities."

Today many investment pundits consider breakthroughs involving the Internet to be on a par with the telephone, the automobile, and electricity. As a result, they believe the standard valuation methods for studying stock prices as taught in business schools simply doesn't apply to the explosion in Internet stocks and other technological innovations. How do you intelligently gauge equities of companies that do not yet make money? The investor must look at factors such as buying patterns, reach, new subscribers, and gross margins, many of today's experts contend, and then mix them together to come up with a "relevant" valuation. Everyone is elated when such a stock eventually does reach a point where its results are in black, not red, ink. That's because the price of a stock compared to its earnings (known as the p/e ratio) still remains the most helpful and down-to-earth tool, as it is based on reality.

Many of today's stocks stumble around in ridiculously oversized valuations that may take years to justify, if ever. Each time they fall down, they pull millions of investors, their money, and the market with them. Yet pricing of many stocks, sometimes based on hopes, dreams, and a little magic dust, often bears little resemblance to reality.

Volatility leaves no new industry segment completely untouched, and this is exacerbated by the fact that there's a greater number of novice traders these days. If you're new to stock trading, follow these common-sense guidelines:

- ✦ Carefully differentiate among companies within a hot industry or industry segment and decide how much they're really worth.

- ✦ Do you understand what a company you're considering really does? Too many investors take the word of a broker or a research report and put money into something they don't understand.

- ✦ Decide whether you have the personal fortitude to endure wild price swings. The euphoria of a 300 percent first-day initial public offering (IPO) gain is often followed by a severe price correction later.

- ✦ Get your feet wet in any new field by investing in a stock mutual fund. Some funds specifically emphasize various segments of technology, but most broad-based mutual funds include many tech stocks as well. Always take a careful look at a fund's holdings by industry group before you invest. Too many investors wind up over-invested in some areas because they don't know what their diversified funds actually hold in their portfolios.

Aiming for the future is even more fun today than it was in Twain's day and rewards can be astonishing; but with so many speculative opportunities available, it's also considerably more risky. Internet funds have been hot tickets, but they have inherent volatility.

The top Internet stock funds in annualized return over the three-year period ending with the first quarter of 2000 (only three were around that long), according to Morningstar, were:

- ✦ Internet Fund; $1,000 minimum initial investment; no-load (no initial sales charge); 800-386-3999; three-year annualized return 144 percent.

- ✦ Munder NetNet Fund—Class A; $250 minimum; 5.5 percent load; 800-438-5789; three-year annualized return 115 percent.

- ✦ WWW Internet Fund; $2,000 minimum initial investment; no-load; 888-263-2204; three-year annualized return 79 percent.

7
DON'T BANK ON
YOUR BANK

"A banker is a person who lends you his umbrella when the sun is shining and wants it back the minute it rains."

Pessimism about the world of banking stems from Mark Twain's personal experience. The publishing firm he owned, Charles L. Webster & Company, went bankrupt after a stock market collapse, and national panic made it impossible to find investors to bail him out of his $160,000 in debt. In the same vein, Twain's father had died virtually bankrupt, leaving the family in poverty. So it should come as no surprise that the specter of bankruptcy and the image of a struggling pauper are common in many of Twain's stories, among them *The Gilded Age* and *Pudd'nhead Wilson*. Yet Twain himself never had to claim personal bankruptcy. He averted it through his own determination and the understanding of creditors who genuinely liked and admired him. He managed to revive his sagging finances with an around-the-world lecture tour in 1895–96 and paid off all creditors in full—a move that added to his national stature as a man of honor.

Today, as in Twain's day, bank borrowers must have their act together. When you apply for a general-purpose loan, you not only want to be approved, but approved at a good rate:

+ Go first to your own bank, since having multiple accounts could sway it in your favor. The more of your business it has, the more it likes you. Stick with someone you know unless the rate difference is substantial.

+ Make sure the rate you're receiving is competitive. You can do this by making some telephone calls or by going online to check out terms of various institutions. Take your time and compare carefully. Too often the borrower is so excited to be approved or to get the opportunity for which the money is intended that caution is thrown to the wind.

+ If you're in a strong financial position, you may be able to bargain the rate down a bit. Now, as always, money talks.

+ Going beyond banks, you may obtain more favorable terms from savings and loan associations or, in the case of smaller loans, from credit unions. There are also loan brokers who can gather several competitive bids for you.

+ There are many other possible vehicles for borrowing, such as home equity, insurance, and company 401(k) retirement plans. Weigh each carefully against the other.

✦ Be absolutely certain that you can swing the pay-off on the loan that you intend to take out. Just the fact that you were granted the loan doesn't necessarily mean that you're in the greatest shape to deal with it. You know yourself and your habits best. The proof of the pudding is in the paying.

Don't get into such debt that you won't have anything left for financial emergencies, and never get deeply into debt for luxury items you could easily do without. If you have trouble meeting your loan demands, talk frankly with the lender. It wants communication so that it can still get repaid over the long haul. A credit counselor can also help you get your finances in order and work out a payment plan.

If your debt exceeds your annual income and is growing faster than your earning potential, you may have to consider the legal action of bankruptcy. In a Chapter 7 liquidation bankruptcy, most assets are sold to repay debts, with a court-appointed trustee overseeing the settling of credit claims. A Chapter 11 or 13 reorganization bankruptcy requires working with the court and creditors to formulate a plan to pay off some or all of the debt over a set time period. Chapter 7 and 13 bankruptcies are generally for individuals, while businesses file under Chapter 11. Although bankruptcy can prevent the loss of your home and provide legal protection from creditors, it greatly damages your credit history and ties you up with the courts. Whether or not you agree with Twain about the character of bankers, bankruptcy should be viewed as a last resort and never entered into lightly.

TOM BACKS HIS STATEMENT

The Adventures of Tom Sawyer

8

THE LAW OF AVERAGES EVENTUALLY MAKES YOU RIGHT

> "A man who goes around with a prophecy-gun ought never to get discouraged; if he will keep up his heart and fire at everything he sees, he is bound to hit something by and by."

In today's volatile financial markets, one "expert" or another is always laying claim to having predicted one significant market turn or another, or having singled out the stocks destined to be leaders. This claim can indeed be true in some cases, but perhaps for only a period of a few weeks or months, maybe only days. Some pundits live off one good call or one good year throughout their entire careers. These people repeatedly appear on the air and in the press, spouting predictions and making recommendations with no one taking them to task later for their misfires. The impression is given that you'll double or triple your money with little risk if only you heed them. There are hundreds of investment letters offering advice on stocks, averaging about $150 for an annual subscription. A few cost many hundreds of dollars. They've also invaded the Internet, with online versions of existing publications as well as entirely new entities.

Some newsletter editors are highly accomplished, with years of successful advice under their belts, while others have little to recommend them. They simply have the wherewithal to put out a publication and consistently make promises they can't keep. In a number of cases, the results they advertise don't even take into account the brokerage commissions required in their buying and selling, which can be a major factor in fast-trading portfolios. Their investment suggestions are often difficult to fathom and they later try to read into them whatever actually transpired in the markets or to individual stocks.

Of course, investors themselves are quite fickle, moving from one hot sheet to another in the hope that the next will conjure up stronger, more up-to-date investment magic. Such constant subscriber movement leads to great consternation on the part of reputable newsletter editors, reminiscent of the lament of the main character Hank Morgan in *A Connecticut Yankee in King Arthur's Court* when the townspeople became interested in a rival magician: "Observe how much a reputation was worth in such a country. These people had seen me do the very showiest bit of magic in history and the only one within their memory that had a positive value, and yet here they were, ready to take up with an adventurer who could offer no evidence of his powers but his mere unproven word."

If you're considering shelling out money for the words of investment newsletters, keep the following in mind:

◆ No one is right all the time, so it's important to check out the long-term results of any newsletter. The *Hulbert Financial Digest* (5051B Backlick Road, Annandale, Va. 22003 or www.hulbertdigest.com) tracks a mythical $10,000 investment and how it has grown or decreased based on each newsletter's recommendations. It's worth consulting to determine whether a newsletter is worth its salt.

◆ Take a trial subscription before committing to any publication. There are often short-term fee subscriptions or low introductory rates. Follow the recommendations during the trial period and see how they do.

◆ Determine whether a particular newsletter shares your individual investment philosophy or goals. If you're a conservative senior citizen looking for stable income investments, a razzle-dazzle micro-cap stock guru won't be for you.

◆ Ask yourself whether the advice in the newsletter is clear and concise, offering a real course of action. If it's blurry and full of platitudes rather than specifics, it's not worth it.

◆ Compare newsletters so you don't overlap similar information. If two newsletters are telling you pretty much the same thing and giving similar recommendations, pick the one you like best.

◆ Don't subscribe to any newsletter that represents or accepts advertising from the companies whose stock it recommends. For obvious reasons, such advice cannot be trusted.

The Wall Street Journal regularly pits the recommendations of investment advisors against stock selections chosen by simply tossing darts at the stock listings. Sometimes the darts win. In the same manner, sometimes even the worst investment letters are capable of sometimes winning. This indicates that you should learn to regularly consult a number of different investment sources, whether newsletters, periodicals, columns, televised reports, financial planners, or brokers. Take into account all this advice, but make the final decisions yourself. Never blindly follow one source and then try to blame that source when things go wrong. The ultimate responsibility rests with you. The prophesy-gun Twain writes about can fool you.

The top-performing investment letters based on five-year annualized returns through February 2000, from 104 newsletters monitored by the *Hulbert Financial Digest,* were:

- ✦ *OTC Insight,* Jim Collins editor; focus on Nasdaq-listed growth stocks; Walnut Creek, California; 800-955-9566; five-year annualized return 70 percent.

- ✦ *Medical Technology Stock Letter,* Jim McCamant editor; focus on biotechnology companies; Berkeley, California; 510-843-1857; five-year annualized return 56 percent.

- ✦ *The Pure Fundamentalist,* Alvin Toral editor; focus on fundamental stock picking; Hammond, Indiana; 800-233-5922; five-year annualized return 48 percent.

- ✦ *MPT Review,* Louis Navellier editor; focus on modern portfolio theory stock-picking; Reno, Nevada; 800-454-1395; five-year annualized return 40 percent.

- ✦ *All Star Fund Trader,* Ron Rowland editor; focus on sector and concentrated mutual fund rotation; Austin, Texas; 800-299-4223; five-year annualized return 39 percent.

9
INSURE FOR SUCCESS

"Certainly there is no nobler field for human effort than the insurance line of business—especially accident insurance. Ever since I have been a director in an accident insurance company I have felt that I am a better man. Life has seemed more precious. Accidents have assumed a kindlier aspect. Distressing special providences have lost half their horror. I look upon a cripple now, with affection and interest—as an advertisement. I do not seem to care for poetry any more. I do not care for politics, even agriculture does not excite me. But to me, now, there is a charm about a railway collision that is unspeakable."

Mark Twain delivered speeches to groups of every imaginable stripe, from osteopaths to the Women's Press Club, from college alumni to captains of industry. He once even made a speech introducing an upstart 26-year-old war correspondent named Winston Churchill at New York's Waldorf-Astoria to a group that was none-too-happy with Britain's involvement in the

Boer War. Living his later years in Connecticut, hub of the insurance world, it is little wonder that Twain would wind up serving as director of an insurance company and talking about that industry at a Hartford dinner speech. While obviously jesting about being entranced by railway collisions, his humor underscores the general uneasiness felt by most Americans when it comes to insurance. It is, after all, an industry that bets that bad things won't happen to you, while you bet your money that they will!

Everyone needs some type of protection from loss, yet too many people these days pay too much for their insurance and don't even wind up with coverage that meets their specific needs. Whatever type of insurance you're considering, be certain that all foreseeable areas of risk are fully covered in your policy. Keep in mind that there are frequently gaps or inadequacies in coverage for personal liability, long-term disability, or valuable personal possessions such as jewelry. Carefully go over any policy's limits before signing it, and adjust your coverage as needed to adapt to any changes that may occur in your family or to your lifestyle. Due to the spirited competition for your insurance dollar and the many different venues for buying insurance, you can enjoy significant savings if you shop around for coverage and select policy features carefully.

Pay attention to these important considerations when buying insurance:

◆ Never buy any policy simply because it came to you directly in the mail. No matter how flashy the advertisement or the spokesperson or how important the letter says you are, what really matters is the financial strength of the insurer. Compare the premiums and terms with other policies, including what's available from your current insurance company.

◆ Check the financial health of the insurance company as gauged by the appropriate rating agencies. Insurance firms tend to sound alike with impressive names, yet some have experienced significant financial trouble in recent years. Choose one you know will be with you for the long haul.

◆ Look for discounts that are given for buying all of your insurance coverage, from car to homeowners to umbrella policies, from the same company. This also makes it easier to keep track of your policies through your agent.

◆ To save hundreds of dollars, look into raising the deductibles on your car, home, or renter's insurance policies. But don't try to save money by skimping on coverage, since an underinsured loss can be disastrous.

If you shop well, your insurance can be a reasonably priced safety net protecting family and possessions. It's unlikely that accidents will "take on a kindlier aspect," as Twain humorously put it, but you can at least count on improved peace of mind.

"AIN'T THAT WORK?"

The Adventures of Tom Sawyer

10
MAKE ALL WORK SEEM LIKE PLAY

> "He (Tom Sawyer) had discovered a great law of human action, without knowing it—namely, that in order to make a man or a boy covet a thing, it is only necessary to make the thing difficult to attain. If he had been a great and wise philosopher, like the writer of this book, he would now have comprehended that work consists of whatever a body is obliged to do, and that Play consists of whatever a body is not obliged to do."
>
> *(The Adventures of Tom Sawyer)*

When Tom Sawyer's buddy Ben Rogers dropped by to make fun of him for being hard at work whitewashing a fence, Tom pretended to be enjoying himself:

"Hello, old chap, you got to work, hey?"
"What do you call work?"
"Why, ain't that work?"
"Well, maybe it is and maybe it ain't. All I know is, it suits Tom Sawyer. . . . Does a boy get to whitewash a fence every day?"

Of course, as Mark Twain's most famous tale continues, soon Ben was begging Tom to let *him* do the whitewashing. Mark Twain ponders the relationship between work and play throughout his writing and speeches. He confessed: "What work I have done I have done because it has been play. If it had been work I shouldn't have done it." He also pointed out that, "When we talk about the great workers of the world we really mean the great players of the world." To his way of thinking, writing wasn't really work at all, but rather like playing an enjoyable parlor game throughout his life.

Investing is a game to many people today, albeit a game with major implications for one's financial well-being. In the old days, investing was considered a necessary if dull exercise. Now there are a lot of cool gadgets, software, online sites, and glossy investment periodicals. Employ a little child psychology on yourself as you use all this neat stuff:

✦ Have fun investing. Keep track of your successes and failures and prepare yourself for portfolio management as though you were getting in shape for the tennis finals at Wimbledon or the seventh game of baseball's World Series.

✦ Enjoy learning more about companies and investment vehicles. Each company has a story, whether it's a good, bad, or boring one. It's up to you to find out what it is and see if that story can translate to dollars.

✦ Follow investments in the same way you'd follow sports, gourmet cooking, or movies. Simply by keeping up on them weekly, you'll build greater interest that will inspire you to follow your holdings and find new ones.

◆ Talk about investing with others. You'll soon find yourself in the same sorts of good-natured disagreements that surround politics or artwork. You don't have to open up your personal portfolio to the world in order to talk money.

◆ Reward yourself for your successes. Don't make investing a drudgery that ultimately leads only to retirement or a large bundle for your heirs. If your investment "work" has made you a little richer, enjoy a night out or a trip to savor those results. You deserve it.

Always stop and smell the roses. If you're lucky you may lose track of where work ends and play begins!

"OBJECT-LESSONS" IN ENGLISH HISTORY.

The Prince and the Pauper

11
GOING FOR BROKER CAN TAKE MANY FORMS

"I consider that a broker goes according to the instincts that are in him, and means no harm, and fulfills his mission according to his lights, and has a right to live, and be happy in a general way, and be protected by the law to some extent, just the same as a better man. I consider that brokers come into the world with souls—I am satisfied they do; and if they wear them out in the course of a longer career of stock-jobbing, have they not a right to come in at the eleventh hour and get themselves half-soled, like old boots, and be saved at last?"

(Daniel in the Lion's Den—and Out Again All Right)

Brokers: Love 'em or leave 'em. To Mark Twain, the stock broker was the gatekeeper of the market, guiding investors toward good or bad purchases. He only begrudgingly acknowledged that these all-powerful financial folks were born with souls, an indication of his loathing for them. He also said in regard to brokers that, "I have been told by a friend, whose judgment I respect, that they are not any more unprincipled than they look."

Times have changed in the brokerage industry, however, because there are more choices. Modern stock investors can select between traditional brokers—who offer advice but charge higher commissions—versus discount and online brokers (often one and the same) who conduct transactions and charge less. Your choice depends not only on how much you're willing to spend, but what kind of service you require. The hours of the major stock exchanges have also expanded, and there are after-hours electronic communications networks that make it possible to trade at your convenience.

Choose a full-service broker if you need help with decisions or need some hand-holding, and are willing to pay for it. The relationship between a full-service broker and the customer can be teacher and pupil, or battling adversaries, each convinced they know the best use of investment cash. A broker who has been informed that you wish a stable, conservative portfolio will be less likely to call you with every hot new tip. Similarly, if you have told your broker you are willing to accept some risks, the two of you can communicate regularly to take advantage of changing opportunities.

When dealing with a full-service broker:

◆ Talk over how often you may be likely to ask for specific information. If you telephone simply out of routine or nervousness, you may be cutting into time your broker could better spend going over his firm's research or otherwise monitoring the market.

◆ Don't allow yourself to be pressed or bullied. After all, it is your money. If you feel that you need a bit more time to decide, take it. If you weren't confident about making a snap decision, you probably made the best decision by waiting. There will be other deals in the future.

◆ Never look to anyone as your total investment guru. Neither you nor your broker should shoulder all the blame or take all the credit.

◆ Decide whether your broker is knowledgeable, has a philosophy that coincides with yours, is understanding of your goals, and isn't just pushing you toward his firm's designated investment picks of the month.

If you're a do-it-yourselfer by nature, discount brokers offer trades at considerably lower cost than full-service brokers, often half the price. Offering no advice on investments, they simply handle transactions. However, most do make available research materials on stocks provided by various analytic firms. Finding the least expensive discount broker is not an easy task, for charges vary with the transaction and each discounter's scale is slightly different from the other's. It is important to get a price based on the specific buying or selling that you wish to do, or the type of transactions you'd be most likely to make with a discount firm if you intend on opening an ongoing account. Though some advertisements depict the buying of stocks as a rote task quickly learned by some sort of osmosis, there's more to it than that. A basic knowledge of how the market works is absolutely necessary.

Online trading is growing with all the speed of the Internet, boosted by inducements such as signing rewards, frequent flyer miles, and telephone service discounts. Commission charges are often phenomenally low, just a fraction of the usual discount broker fees. Only invest online if you're confident that the firm you're interested in has the services you require and the capacity to keep up with the demands of a gyrating, high-volume stock market. You may still find yourself complaining loudly on record trading days about just how low-tech a high-tech industry can seem as you wait and wait to make a trade or obtain necessary information. The online field includes some of the biggest discount firms, as well as smaller strictly online firms. In addition, full-service brokers have been introducing online divisions.

According to the Gomez.com research firm, the best online brokers, based on criteria that included ease of use, customer confidence, on-site resources, and overall cost as of the first quarter of 2000 are:

1. Charles Schwab
2. E*Trade
3. DLJdirect
4. Fidelity Investments
5. NDB
6. A.B. Watley
7. My Discount Broker
8. American Express Brokerage
9. Suretrade
10. Morgan Stanley Dean Witter.

When selecting an online broker:

◆ Always check the stipulations on the lowest-priced trades. Not every deal is quite as good as it sounds.

✦ Realize that services vary from basic trading to multiple features and that each firm has its own particular business targets. Some online brokers want to provide a personal finance destination with all kinds of personal finance products and tools readily available to customers, while others are purely brokerages.

✦ Be aware that all online brokers have received complaints about lack of efficiency on record trading days, though some have fared better than others. New accounts have simply been coming in too fast to keep up effectively.

✦ Computer hackers have succeeded in disrupting service of online brokers. Firms are improving their security procedures, but this is still likely to occur from time to time, with varying severity.

This is not your father's brokerage industry. Whether or not Twain really did believe that a broker "has a right to live" and "can be saved at last," his admiration of technology and new ideas makes it easy to imagine a modern-day Twain busily tapping on his computer keys on the way to making a quick online purchase of a hot new stock. Common sense investing, but using a newfangled approach—it makes perfect sense.

A KING, POOR FELLOW!

The Adventures of Tom Sawyer

12

DON'T TURN YOUR FINANCES INTO A GAME OF CHANCE

"A dollar picked up in the road is more satisfaction to you than the ninety-and-nine which you had to work for, and money won at faro or in stocks snuggles into your heart in the same way."

"At the Shrine of St. Wagner"

Faro, derived from the Egyptian word *pharaoh,* is a gambling game in which players bet on cards drawn from a dealing box. It was especially popular in the 1800s, and many modern films that depict the Old West have featured faro dealers in their town saloons. Mark Twain, who loved to play all kinds of card games also enjoyed billiards, easily equated cards with stock gains or found money. All three, in his eyes, can be considerably more fun than money derived from a hard-earned paycheck.

Effort is always required to change stock investing from a game of chance to a systematic way to build financial security. When you're buying a stock, it's a lot like buying a business. Your small piece reflects the total company, which means you must look at all aspects of that company, not just the more exciting or obvious aspects of it. Pfizer Corp. is more than its Viagra treatment for impotency, Walt Disney Co. is more than theme parks, and Estee Lauder is more than simply the single Estee Lauder brand. Japan's Ito-Yokado owns thousands of 7-Eleven stores in the U.S., while the U.K.'s Bass Plc. brewer owns thousands of Holiday Inns. Too many investors plunk money down on a stock because they're attracted to some single aspect of a company, rather than analyzing the whole entity. Or, they neglect to keep up with the many changes companies have undergone. More importantly, they aren't aware of how stocks differ significantly.

Unlike a game of cards, you actually have an opportunity to choose the stocks in your deck:

+ Blue-chip stocks are well-known, quality companies such as General Electric. They've been leaders in their industries for years and boast a solid track record that appeals to risk-averse conservative investors.

+ Growth stocks represent companies that have greater potential to increase their sales, earnings, and stock price than most other companies or the economy in general. Computer networking company Cisco Systems is an excellent example of this type of intelligently aggressive firm.

+ Small-cap stocks are higher-risk emerging companies whose growth patterns indicate they could become leaders in the market. They're not there yet, so you're making a bet they will be one day. Mid-cap stocks are the next step up in size before blue chips.

◆ Income stocks feature generation of income as their goal, therefore pay higher dividends to attract conservative investors. Electric utilities are a good example of the type of stock that seniors on fixed incomes might prefer.

◆ Value stocks have better prospects than their stock prices indicate. They're bargains, though not down and out. After all, buying a stock cheaply and selling after it has appreciated in price is the ultimate goal of every investor.

Want to raise the stakes a bit? Speculative stocks, such as those representing the high-tech or biotech companies, have greater risk and their prices are much higher than their financial results would indicate. They often have no earnings whatsoever, just a belief that they're poised for explosive growth. Additional investment opportunities, so-called penny or micro-cap stocks, sell for $5 or less a share and are undeniably volatile. They're best for aggressive investors capable of rolling with the punches. While speculative stocks require that you do your homework in order to choose effectively, investors often make snap decisions based on "hot tips" and scant information. Chosen casually and without advice or research, you'd be much better off playing the sort of high-stakes card game with which Twain was familiar.

Measuring the size of companies has become a bit more free-form. Market capitalization, the value of a company determined by the market price of its issued and outstanding stock, has always been the most common way to gauge a company's size. These days there are no longer universally accepted breakpoints for determining small-, mid-, or large-cap stocks because the inflated prices of the past several years have changed the rules. Previously, anything less than $1 billion was small cap and anything more than $5 billion was large cap. However, the Russell 2000, a small-cap index, now has many stocks with more than $1.5 billion in market capitalization; large-cap stocks have market capitalizations of $11 billion or more; and mid-caps have market caps from $1.7 billion to $10.7 billion. The investor must still consider the relative size of companies, but they can no longer be shoved so easily as pegs into holes.

Incidentally, while Twain did greatly enjoy gambling, he despised opera and especially the operas of German composer Richard Wagner. He believed no one would ever enjoy such music naturally. His dollar-picked-up-in-the-road quote came from "At the Shrine of St. Wagner," which described a distasteful (for Twain) visit to Germany to hear the Wagner opera *Parsifal* at a festival Wagner had founded. In his autobiography, Twain happily quoted another humorist who said "Wagner's music is better than it sounds."

13
THANK YOU VERY MUCH FOR YOUR INTEREST

> "Pap always said it warn't no harm to borrow things, if you was meaning to pay them back, sometime; but the widow said it warn't anything but a soft name for stealing."
>
> *Adventures of Huckleberry Finn*

Huck Finn, that fun-loving outcast hero who didn't enjoy book-learnin' much or practice fancy manners, did indeed do some "borrowing" from time to time. His Pap, a no-account drunk who'd abandoned his son, certainly offered little moral foundation upon which to build. In *Adventures of Huckleberry Finn,* the abusive father holds Huck hostage in an isolated cabin in an attempt to obtain money from him. The honorable Mark Twain's own borrowing, however, was strictly on the up and up. It involved creditors who backed his various publishing efforts, and the unsuccessful development of a complicated automatic typesetting machine, the Paige compositor, which forced his firm into bankruptcy during a period of nationwide financial panic and few government safeguards. In his later years, he got expert advice and worked his way back on top financially, but maintained a cynical attitude toward the modern concept of credit that was most likely due to his own problems with it.

Credit has exploded in popularity since Twain's time. Americans today are world-leading borrowers, to a level never envisioned, and the pitfalls remain great. The typical modern family is lugging around a steamer trunk of credit card debt. Card issuers offer easy credit in mass mailings that tout incredibly low short-term "teaser" rates. Once those rates expire, the issuers gouge consumers with high rates that go on for years. Card rates remain lofty when other rates are low; they escalate even higher at the hint of any general rate movement. It's unlikely you'll be able to offset with investment return the hefty charge you're paying on a typical revolving credit account. Most of the profit gains card issuers now enjoy come from higher fees and penalty charges. Late payment fees, charges for exceeding credit limits, and higher rates as penalty for late payment are all rising rapidly. Five years ago, less than half the major card issuers imposed penalties, while now more than 90 percent of them do.

The best investment you can make is to pay off your credit debt. The costs you'll ultimately save in interest will help you put money into investment vehicles that can help the long-term well-being of your family. Investors with heavy debt loads often feel compelled to take on higher risks in their investing strategy to try to make up the difference. This just doesn't work. If paying everything off is not immediately possible, try to systematically whittle down your outstanding debt bill each month. Cut back on the number of credit cards you own, leave most of those you do own at home, and seek out the best card deals. A number of generally-available low-rate card deals have rates 6 or 7 percent lower than the average. Unless you intend to pay them off in full each month, avoid department store credit cards like the plague because they charge the very highest rates of all. It's a double-whammy: You spend too much on merchandise and then pay through the nose to finance it all.

Twain worked hard to repay each and every one of his creditors in full in order to avoid personal bankruptcy. None of us can be smart all the time, but at least we can be honorable. Don't turn into a scoundrel just because you feel your creditors are unworthy. Here is some advice for handling credit-card accounts:

- ✦ If you have trouble paying off your credit card bills, don't hide from lenders or lie about a "check in the mail." This irritates them greatly.

- ✦ Talk it over with creditors and work up a viable payment plan. They simply want to hear that you intend to make good. Running away is the surest way to ruin your credibility and credit record, thereby increasing the likelihood that the creditors will contact your employer and go after your paycheck.

- ✦ If you really need help, there are credit counseling services to help you get back on track. They'll help you work out a plan with creditors and perhaps pay off some bills first. The bottom line to avoiding credit problems is to have a budget and follow it.

- ✦ When shopping for items, set your spending limits in advance. You might also bring only one or two of your cards with you.

Now that's common sense, but temptation too often overcomes common sense.

14

IN CURRENCY WE TRUST

> "Some men worship rank, some worship heroes,
> some worship power, some worship God, and over
> these ideals they dispute and cannot unite—but they
> all worship money."

The power of money was always a Mark Twain fascination and he often depicted its powerful impact on people's lives. In his short story "The 1,000,000-Pound Bank-Note," a penniless young mining-broker clerk is given a million-pound bank note by two eccentric, elderly brothers who made bets with each other on what would happen to a stranger wandering about with no cash and only such a note. The young man is loaned the note interest-free for 30 days. Although the note is not legal tender, everyone he encounters is in awe of what it represents and gladly provide him wardrobe, lodging, and whatever else he requires. He gains fame in the gossip columns and, by lending his good name to another man's plan to sell mining options, earns a fortune in his own right. At the story's conclusion, he winds up marrying the stepdaughter of one of the two old men. In other words, the very appearance of having money is enough to bring this money-worshiping world to one's feet!

Human nature hasn't changed. In today's world, the appearance of money is still all-important to many people. As one advertising campaign for a popular camera put it: "Image is everything!" The amount of money that individuals put down to buy homes continues to dwindle, car leasing has replaced ownership for many, credit card balances revolve endlessly, and the look of casual wealth is enthusiastically emulated. Having the "right" membership or address still brings cache because others are confident this connotes plenty of money. In the 1983 film *Trading Places,* street person Eddie Murphy is exchanged for well-to-do broker Dan Akyroyd as part of a wager by two elderly brothers. The 1994 film *A Million to Juan* starred Paul Rodriguez as a street vendor who was given a check for $1 million for one month by a wealthy man in a limousine. Both plot lines owe much to "The 1,000,000-Pound Bank-Note," and prove that Twain's message about our shallow attitude toward wealth remains relevant today.

15

HE WHO HESITATES CAN SAVE A LOT MORE

"Simple rules for saving money: To save half, when you are fired by an eager impulse to contribute to charity, wait and count forty. To save three-quarters, count sixty. To save it all, count sixty-five."

Following the Equator

There's really no need to be uncharitable to save effectively, as this tongue-in-cheek comment from Mark Twain's last travel book advises. You can simply do the "hesitation counting" whenever you're about to buy an impulse item at the local department store or spend a little too much on a night out. The more you think through how you'll spend money, the less money you're likely to spend.

It's important to formulate a thoughtful family budget and stick with it. Start by carefully observing exactly how much you're actually spending, including the pocket cash that some folks seem to forget about. You can use a simple ledger or a financial software package to track your habits accurately. Calculate the percentage of your income that goes to various expenditures. For example, it's best if no more than two-thirds of your monthly income goes for necessities such as food, utilities, and housing. Also try to keep monthly bills for car and credit installments under 10 percent of your income. Once you've got all the numbers, you can assess where you're spending too much and where you may be able to cut back. Also go over past tax returns to track what's coming and going. Formulate a realistic family budget that you'll be able to follow and still have some luxuries so you can enjoy life.

It's much easier to save when you've got some specific goals of varying lengths of time, such as a vacation, a car, educating the children, or retiring. Once you figure them out, you can set a disciplined path toward meeting them. "Make it a point to do something every day that you don't want to do," Twain wrote. "This is the golden rule for acquiring the habit of doing your duty without pain." But the real key to the rigors of saving is to realize how important it is to save regularly. All that talk about the miracles of compounding is true. If you can have an automatic deduction each month put into your savings account, you'll be amazed at how quickly your savings will mount up. Financial planners call this "paying yourself first." And the sooner you save, the better. For example, a $100 monthly deposit with an 8 percent return would grow over the course of 10 years to $18,417; over 20 years to $59,295; and over 40 years to $351,428. When you save automatically, you don't notice you're saving and the long-term results can be astounding. Of course, you can't just toss your money into anything. It's important to balance the merits of yield, liquidity, and safety in your investment choices.

Always make sure you're getting the best deals possible when you save:

+ Shop several banks and financial institutions to see which offers the best interest with the lowest potential fees on basic banking products and automated teller services. Consider your own needs and banking routine in doing this.

+ Find out whether banking online can save you money. Many banks have instituted attractive programs to encourage electronic banking.

+ When you move into investment products, find out which of the best-performing mutual funds have the lowest fees and which stock brokers have the most reasonable transaction charges.

+ Discount brokers and online brokers who charge less than the full-service brokers who offer advice have become popular with do-it-yourself investors, but you must know what you're doing before taking this important step. You won't receive any hand-holding.

If you save wisely through a well-engineered program that takes into account your needs, you should amass more than enough money so you can readily help out your favorite charity when it comes calling. When you donate to charity, be sure that you get receipts. If you donate personal possessions such as clothing or furniture, you can take a deduction for the property's fair market value. Document all donations for tickets to charitable events (be careful, though—in the case of a dinner event, the actual price of the meal is *not* deductible).

One especially good idea is to donate stock to the charity, since you won't have to pay capital gains tax on the profits and the full value of the stock can be deducted as a charitable donation. You can also have an accountant or tax attorney help you set up a charitable remainder trust. In that case, the charity accepts your gift of assets, sells them, and invests the proceeds, paying you an income stream for either a specific number of years or for your lifetime.

16
MISSED OPPORTUNITIES CAN COME BACK TO HAUNT YOU

"There was a young fellow there who said that he had been a reporter on a Providence newspaper but that he was in another business now. He was with Graham Bell and was agent for a new invention called the telephone. He believed there was great fortune in store for it and wanted me to take some stock. I declined. I said I didn't want anything more to do with wildcat speculation. Then he offered the stock to me at twenty-five. I said I didn't want it at any price. He became eager—insisted that I take five hundred dollars' worth. He said he would sell me as much as I wanted for five hundred dollars—offered to let me gather it up in my hands and measure it in a plug hat—said I could have a whole hatful for five hundred dollars. But I was the burnt child and I resisted all these temptations, resisted them easily, went off with my check intact. . . ."

(The Autobiography of Mark Twain)

To Mark Twain's credit, he was always willing to acknowledge his mistakes and missed opportunities. In this particular situation, he had a check burning a hole in his pocket, yet decided to leave it there.

He took the prudent course rather than investing on something new and risky. The fact that he was a technology buff and quickly grew to love the new invention called the telephone, probably only rubbed salt into his wound later. That $500 investment would've made a fortune.

These days, the speculative buzz is over initial public offerings, or IPOs, as privately-held companies issue shares to become publicly traded. This gives the company the opportunity to raise money and the founding shareholders the opportunity to sell their stock at a high price. An underwriting investment banking firm makes a bundle for handling the financial arrangements of the IPO. At the front of the line to buy IPOs are institutional investors such as mutual funds, pension plans, and brokerage firms. The underwriting firm's best customers get an early shot at IPOs as well, leaving the average investors with scant opportunity.

New IPO wealth is being enjoyed in the most unexpected of places. Britain's Queen Elizabeth II made about $1.5 million on the public offering of Getmapping.com Plc. in 2000. She'd invested $160,000 the year before for a 1.5 percent stake in the company, which is taking aerial photographs of all of Britain. Her resulting stake in this dot-com company after the IPO was more than nine times her initial investment. Not bad for someone who took up investing for herself late in life.

If you're thinking of investing in an IPO but don't have a palace or royal jewelry to fall back on, keep this in mind:

- ◆ The track record of a hot IPO is usually a tremendous price jump early on, to be followed by a downturn as the sizzle disappears and investors who made big money head for the exits.

✦ Some IPOs have made their financial figures and potential look better than they actually are. In some cases, the numbers a few months down the road will look considerably different from those at the outset.

✦ It's often a better idea to wait until a solid IPO has suffered through its initial downturn, then buy it when it's more reasonably priced on the aftermarket as you'd buy any stock.

✦ Some IPOs are bombs from the very beginning. Their success is hardly universal. The problem could be as basic as being introduced on a bad day for the market or when a similar type of firm is suffering significant, much-publicized problems. You never know.

✦ Since some mutual funds emphasize IPOs and have access to early investment, it might make more sense to invest in one of them. It also spreads your risk, so that you don't have a big bet on only one company.

✦ If you do have the opportunity and decide to invest, always get a copy of an upcoming IPO's preliminary prospectus, or "red herring" (named for the portions in red ink). Study carefully the financial statements, management, growth potential, and rivals before you make a move.

✦ Remember that the price for the IPO won't be set until shortly before the stock is presented to the buying public.

An IPO is a bet. Twain made the mistake of not making a financial bet on Bell stock, but he didn't actually lose any cash out of his pocket. You, on the other hand, could make a bet on an IPO and lose big-time.

TRAVELING BY RAIL.

Adventures of Huckleberry Finn

17

CHECK WHERE YOU'VE BEEN BEFORE YOU GO ANYWHERE

"Few of us can stand prosperity. Another man's, I mean."

(Pudd'nhead Wilson)

Many people are jealous of what seem to be the obscene investment profits enjoyed by others in our society. Similarly, the *nouveau riche* of Mark Twain's era bagged the first spoils of a modern mercantilist era, their extravagant lifestyles making the lives of the have-nots appear to be even further behind. Twain would often portray himself as a common man aspiring to the high life. "I have always made it a rule to have the best of everything, even if I am obliged to get trusted for it," he wrote in a humorous newspaper article about requesting credit on a visit to New York. "This sterling maxim was instilled in my mind by a kind father; and who shall say that gray-haired old man is not proud of his orphan boy?"

Today aspiration to the good life is even stronger. We've seen an investment shift to a new technological economy, accompanied by new wealth and excesses. Instead of beating yourself up over the good fortune of others, carefully examine the results of the past so that you can make the right moves in the future. A sense of history is in order. Pay attention to the specific stock, its past, its price, its prospects, and any potential pitfalls. Don't fret over whether someone once bought it at a lower price. You may find the best values of all in good companies that have escaped notice in all the hype of the twenty-first century.

Find out where the money was and wasn't made. Over the five-year period through the first quarter of 2000, home prices nationwide had a five-year annualized appreciation of just over 4 percent, while the average price of gold suffered an annualized decline of 6 percent. Art and collectibles revived from their early- to mid-1990s doldrums. Meanwhile, the Standard & Poor's 500's annualized gain of 22 percent beat the S&P SmallCap 600's 17 percent. In mutual funds, the five-year annualized gain for U.S. diversified stocks was 22 percent for the period, while bond funds produced a 5.40 percent annualized return. Although it suffered some precipitous drops along the way, the technology stock group provided a dramatic five-year annualized return of 50 percent. Leaders within that group were computer networking, computer software and semiconductors. Volatile, high-powered tech investing is here to stay and future projections show it to be vibrant and alive. Communications followed with a five-year annualized return of 24 percent, health care 21 percent, and financials 19 percent.

The best-performing stocks in annualized return over the five-year period that ended with the first quarter of 2000 were in tech or biotech:

✦ CMGI (stock symbol CMGI); an online information company; annualized return 198 percent.

✦ Imclone Systems (IMCL); biotechnology firm; annualized return 193 percent.

✦ Qlogic (QLGC); semiconductor company; annualized return 189 percent.

✦ JDS Uniphase (JDSU); phone/network equipment company; annualized return 189 percent.

✦ Veritas Software (VRTS), software firm; annualized return 171 percent.

The Internet revolution made it easy for a number of tech companies without sound fundamentals to do well in the market, but there's always a shakeout of winners and losers. While tech will be a great sector the next five years, it will be increasingly volatile. One of the best ways to invest in technology is through mutual funds, which spread the risk through a portfolio of dozens or hundreds of stocks.

The top sector funds based on five-year annualized returns were big in technology:

✦ Firsthand Technology Value Fund; $10,000 minimum; no load (no sales charge); 888-884-2675; annualized return 68 percent.

✦ PIMCO Innovation Fund—Class A; $2,500 minimum; 5.5 percent load; 800-426-0107; annualized return 59 percent.

✦ Fidelity Select Electronics Portfolio; $2,500 minimum; 3 percent load; 800-544-8888; annualized return 58 percent.

✦ First American Technology Fund—Class A; $1,000 minimum; 5.25 percent front-end load; 800-637-2548; annualized return 56 percent.

✦ Fidelity Select Technology Portfolio; $2,500 minimum; 3 percent front-end load; 800-544-8888; annualized return 54 percent.

The old rules of thumb that investment strategists have used to determine whether the market is overvalued are being peeled away. So it makes sense for the investor to continue to look at a company, to know what it is and what it does, and to ask whether it will be around five or ten years from now. Declining dividend yield is traditionally an indicator of future market trouble, and when the average yield on S&P 500 stocks slid below 3 percent in 1994, difficult times were feared. However, the average yield began 2000 at 1.2 percent and many experts decided that it doesn't seem representative of much of anything.

If you fear volatility, the most sublime, low-volatility stocks over five years were:

✦ Mesa Royalty Trust (MTR), which holds royalty interests in oil/gas properties; five-year standard deviation (denoting how far a stock wanders from its average return) of 8.49; annualized return of 9 percent.

✦ Santa Fe Energy Trust (SFF), which holds royalty interests in Santa Fe Energy Resources oil/gas properties; five-year standard deviation of 10.79; annualized return 11 percent.

+ American Insured Mortgage Investors (AIA), a real estate investment trust that invests in insured mortgages; five-year standard deviation of 12.62; annualized return 9 percent.

We've learned from recent history that diversification still matters—and will continue to matter—an idea that got lost in the shuffle of the bull market. For example, small-cap and Japanese stocks had been given up for dead, but had a great showing in 1999. U.S. blue-chip stocks aren't the be-all and end-all of a portfolio, and you need an annual re-balancing of your portfolio to be positioned properly. For example, while value-oriented funds have done poorly, investors should continue to keep the faith. Their time always comes.

The top diversified U.S. stock funds the past five years ending with the first quarter of 2000 were:

+ Rydex Series Trust OTC Fund-Investor Class; large-cap growth fund; $25,000 minimum; no-load; 800-820-0888; annualized return of 57 percent.

+ RS Emerging Growth Fund, small-cap growth fund; $5,000 minimum; no-load; 800-766-3863; annualized return of 52 percent.

+ Fremont U.S. Micro-Cap Fund; small-cap growth fund; $2,000 minimum; no-load; 800-548-4539; annualized return of 48 percent.

+ Fidelity New Millennium Fund; mid-cap growth fund; 3 percent front-end load; 800-544-8888; annualized return 47 percent.

◆ IPS Millennium Fund; large growth fund, $1,000 mini-
  mum, no-load; 800-232-9142; five-year annualized return
  47 percent.

As the investment advertisements must always point out,
past results do not assure future results. But, as you make your
investment selections, keep a sense of history. It helps to know
where you've been as you head forward. With a carefully
chosen portfolio, maybe someday someone will be jealous of
your riches!

18
COMMON SENSE CAN PREVAIL

"Honesty is the best policy—when there is money in it."

With investors constantly searching for the next "new thing," it's easy to overlook honest, common-sense investing that has no secret formulas or crystal balls purported to peer into the future. Many investors have simply thrown the past out the window, but that's foolhardy. Times may change, but they build on the same foundation. Furthermore, it's important to hold some stocks in your portfolio whose financial data and future projections are firmly based on reality, rather than company or brokerage firm propaganda and pure speculation over the future. A company that's been turning out dependable results for years may be one you can count on in a downturn affecting the trendier new offerings.

The beliefs of experts whose philosophies have had staying power must be considered. They always seem to find the bright spot when others can't. "It is easy to find fault, if one has that disposition," Twain wrote in *Puddn'Head Wilson.* "There was once a man who, not being able to find any other fault with coal, complained that there were too many prehistoric toads in it."

The most famous of the traditional market strategists, here listed alphabetically, keep their philosophies relentlessly long-term:

John C. Bogle, who for decades has championed low-cost mutual funds as dynamic leader of the Vanguard Group of mutual funds, believes today's investor should pick an asset allocation model and stick with it. Market timing cannot be done successfully, he contends. In the uncertain world of the new millennium, he recommends a diversified stock portfolio as the most sensible choice. Select the percentages of your portfolio based on your time frame, asset size, necessary income, and your own courage, then stay the course. As part of his lifelong crusade, he urges selecting stocks with low expense ratios, low portfolio turnover, and tax efficiency. If you don't need advice, don't pay for it in the form of sales commissions or sales fees. Carefully use past fund performance to measure consistency and risk, he advises, but not to predict future performance.

Warren Buffett, whose Omaha-based Berkshire Hathaway Inc. money management firm and its stock have turned in remarkable long-term results, considers buying a stock the very same as buying an entire business. Known for his refreshingly candid annual reports and shareholder meetings, Buffett looks for understandable, necessary, unregulated businesses with favorable long-term prospects. He expects management of these firms to be rational and very candid with shareholders, just as he is with his own shareholders. His focus is on return on equity, and he especially admires companies with high profit margins and attractive stock prices, something that's often lacking in the most aggressive technology investing. His lack of tech holdings has taken its toll in certain market periods, but he maintains that his steady approach in the long run will be more dependable than investing in overpriced equities.

Peter Lynch, the successful manager of Fidelity Magellan who left that post in 1990 and is now a highly publicized spokesman for Fidelity Investments, strongly urges buying stocks over bonds. He contends that an amateur who devotes a small amount of study to companies in an industry he or she knows something about can outperform 95 percent of mutual fund managers. In the case of stocks, he believes investors should give special consideration to the stock of companies whose products or services they know and like. When picking a mutual fund, stick with a steady and consistent performer rather than trying to move in and out of funds. Hedge your bets by dividing your money among three or four types of funds, such as growth, value, emerging growth, and capital appreciation, so you won't be left out in the cold when some are under-performing.

With these three investment heroes, what you see is what you get. No matter what your investment philosophy, you can learn from them as you construct and nurture your own portfolio. Diversity and judicious choice of investments are common sense moves that can bolster your finances. "Prosperity is the best protector of principle," Twain noted in *Follow the Equator*.

HUCKLEBERRY FINN

The Adventures of Tom Sawyer

19

KEEP SOME SPARE CHANGE—JUST IN CASE

"Spending one's capital is feeding a dog on its own tail."

The folks who earn the most money or appear to have the most money aren't necessarily the ones who wind up with the most money in the end. Living well until the end of your entire life is the real goal, and dealing effectively with your investments, retirement accounts, and pension over the long haul will make all the difference in the world. It's easy to lose sight of long-term values: In Mark Twain's "The Man that Corrupted Hadleyburg," a stranger makes fools of a town's self-righteous citizens with a hoax in which each attempts to become the winner of $40,000 in gold coins. After these solid citizens lie and cheat to win, the coins turned out to be nothing more than gilded lead slugs. They got nothing for their efforts.

Be sure to make your efforts count. At some point, you'll have to decide how best to cope with inflation, how to take money out of your retirement plans, and when to pay income tax on tax-deferred investments. These must be studied decisions. Capital is any asset used to generate income or make a long-term investment, such as the money you use to buy stock or put a down-payment on your house. Having current income makes sense throughout your entire life, and that means you should have an investment plan in place for obtaining it. Stock, bond, or savings account investments should take income and growth into account so you'll be able to cope with inflation and what is likely to be a long life. To avoid taking from the nest egg, investors should put aside emergency money for any unplanned expenses involving cars, medicine, or vacations. When a couple retires, living expenses don't disappear; travel, shopping, and enjoying the grandchildren can add up financially. And as you age, you're also more likely to have medical needs and you may require additional help at home. To be properly prepared, during your working career you should be sure to have continuous insurance coverage, live beneath your means, avoid debt whenever possible, participate in employee-sponsored retirement plans such as 401(k) plans, and, when changing jobs, roll over any vested pension benefits into an individual retirement plan.

Always sweat the details. Workers often aren't aware of the differences in employer-sponsored pension plans, and that lack of knowledge can affect their planning for the future. Consider these definitions:

+ A *defined-benefit plan* guarantees you a set dollar amount when you retire, taking into account your salary, length of service, or both.

◆ A *defined-contribution plan,* which takes in money from you, your employer, or both, does not guarantee the benefit amount.

◆ A *profit-sharing retirement plan,* funded by the firm and often tied to profits, makes no payment guarantees.

When you retire or exit the company, pension money is paid out either as a lump sum or in regular payments for your lifetime. To avoid the 10 percent penalty on any tax deferred retirement money, you must leave it invested until you reach at least age 59 1/2. Most advisors suggest deferring tax-deferred investment income for as long as possible. Keep in mind that you can't rely on pension and Social Security benefits alone to provide for your retirement.

Before you retire, carefully establish what your retirement income will be and closely estimate the costs of living you'll encounter. Calculate how much you'll need to keep on saving during your retirement years and prepare a plan to meet those needs. As you near retirement, request your Social Security "Personal Earnings and Benefit Statement" and get together the documents required to process your benefits three months in advance. Have your company's human resources department figure exactly how much you'll receive in benefits, how you'll receive them, and when the first check will be sent. Don't leave anything to chance. Don't take big bites out of *capital* that you won't be able to replace. As Twain would suggest, leave that dog in one piece.

WORTH NOTHING.

Roughing It

20

YOUR BUBBLE COULD BURST IF YOU'RE NOT CAREFUL

"I wonder how much it would take to buy a soap-bubble, if there was only one in the world."

(A Tramp Abroad)

But what if it were a soap-bubble to die for? Written as Mark Twain's third travel book, "A Tramp Abroad" told of a trip through Germany and Switzerland in which "brick-a-brack" (collectible) hunting was an important aspect. The American investor today still loves the romance of collectibles, especially those unusual "one-of-a-kind" items uncovered on a trip far away from home. The fact that they have a history adds to their allure. "Let us not be too particular," Twain quipped. "It is better to have second-hand diamonds than none at all."

Collectibles spur the imagination with dreams of riches, encouraged by some truly monumental prices paid for certain pieces at auction, whether Claude Monet paintings, Marilyn Monroe jewelry, Beatles lunchboxes, or autographed Babe Ruth baseball cards. But get real: Only in select cases and with thoughtful planning do collectibles have any positive effect on anyone's pocketbook. Most items won't appreciate, and may actually decline.

Scarcity, condition, and quality are important in evaluating any collectible, but it must still be an item that someone else is willing to buy one day. Gold, diamonds, coins, artwork, antiques, autographs, sports items, and pop memorabilia all go through inevitable cycles and weather inexplicable trends in popularity and unpopularity. Most collectibles are meant to be bought and held, and their value as inflation hedges must take into account hard-to-predict factors that may even include world economic events, such as runaway inflation. Due to all the variables in collecting, it makes the most sense to buy something that you genuinely like. Then, if you develop a passion for it, you'll no doubt become a better long-term collector as well. You'll make the right contacts, it will be less likely that you'll be "taken" by someone disreputable, and you may even unearth some real bargains. And if what you bought goes out of style, you won't consider it to be a weight hanging from your neck.

In all cases, you must realize that you're responsible for safekeeping, that your holding may be hard to sell, or that you may become so attached to it that you never sell it anyway. If a vintage Superman comic or a shiny diamond becomes something you just can't part with, it's not an investment. Maybe your heirs will enjoy it one day (and there's no certainty of that), but it won't bring you a dime during your lifetime.

Nonetheless, if you still consider yourself capable of finding some good deals and love the thrill of the hunt, here are some suggestions so you can shop wisely for collectibles:

◆ Develop an eye for the items yourself, either by visiting museums, dealers, or auction houses. You can easily get information free of charge.

◆ Look into the reputation of the dealer selling the item. Besides word-of-mouth recommendations, credentials from professional organizations can help.

◆ Dealers tend to be retailers, while auctions require homework but offer a chance to shop for the best deals.

◆ To protect your investment, have it evaluated every three years by an appraiser who meets the qualifications for the Internal Revenue Service. You want the value placed on the item to hold up for tax reasons, whether you keep it, sell it, or donate it to charity one day.

◆ Get insurance through a rider to your homeowner's or renter's coverage.

◆ Ask the dealer selling you the item if he will help you sell it in the future.

◆ Buy what you can afford. Going deeply into debt over an illiquid investment is a risk you don't need to assume.

TOM SAWYER'S BAND OF ROBBERS.

Adventures of Huckleberry Finn

21

BIDE YOUR TIME
AND WATCH YOUR
INVESTMENT GROW

"It's no use to throw a good thing away merely because the market isn't ripe yet."

(A Connecticut Yankee in King Arthur's Court)

When exactly is the market ripe for a stock? The sooner you get involved in a company's life cycle, the greater your eventual gain should be once it matures. That could mean there are opportunities in small-company, technology, biotechnology, and telecommunications stocks, so long as you're willing to go through the inevitable growing pains associated with them.

The Nasdaq, variously representing itself as the stock market for the next 100 years and the stock market for the so-called New Economy, prides itself on being a breeding ground for eventual market-leading equities. It is the stock exchange of choice for most companies going public. That's an invigorating concept, but it's also risky at times because the companies don't have enough of a track record to be predictable in unforeseen scenarios. Such companies built on high hopes for the future are also hit the hardest during market declines. It's not unlike Mark Twain's day, when the array of new technological inventions was never-ending, but making a financial bet on which ones were going to succeed could sometimes be a hit-or-miss affair.

Here's what you should know about the volatile Nasdaq, which stands for the National Association of Securities Dealers Automated Quotation System:

- ✦ It was the first electronic-based stock market and, from its creation in 1971, hasn't utilized a traditional trading floor but rather a vast network permitting traders from offices across the country to execute stock transactions.

- ✦ Rapidly gaining prominence, it has been the fastest-growing of the world's major stock markets, with volume that exceeds the New York Stock Exchange.

- ✦ Its 5,500 or so equities are often quite small, though some have grown to gargantuan proportions, among them Cisco Systems, Microsoft, Intel, Oracle, Applied Materials, Sun Microsystems, Dell Computer, and Novell.

- ✦ The Nasdaq Composite Index is often cited as the New Economy gauge, while the Dow Jones industrial average is an Old Economy gauge. That's overstated, since every era's new economy stocks—as was the case with telephone stocks—eventually meld into the larger whole.

Simply being small isn't necessarily a virtue if that small size doesn't also hold promise for the future. A lot of little companies never go anywhere. With so many firms in the technology area, it becomes a bigger and bigger task to try to differentiate among them. A bit of bad news affecting one company can unfairly send the entire index into a tizzy because not all investors are sophisticated enough to tell immediately how individual companies will be influenced by the news.

It's also worth knowing the other major stock indexes so that you can compare the performance of your stock with others in its category, or invest in an index mutual fund that meets your needs:

+ The Dow Jones Industrial Average, created by Charles Dow in 1896, tracks performance of thirty of the biggest U.S. companies, including General Electric and General Motors. GE is the only remaining stock from the original list. The stocks of Microsoft and Intel were among those most recently added to represent changes in the economy. "What's the Dow doing?" is still a familiar daily query, though its prominence has slipped in comparison to the Nasdaq and Standard & Poor's 500. There are other Dow indexes for specific industries, such as transportation and utilities.

+ The Standard & Poor's 500 is a broader market measure featuring 500 companies primarily traded on the NYSE. It was a red-hot performer in the second half of the 1990s, with the index mutual funds that replicate its holdings turning in strong returns. Many experts recommend it as a "no-brainer" way to play the market.

+ The Wilshire 5000 is the very broadest of the market indexes, with more than 6,000 American companies from the major exchanges. It tracks broad stock-market trends.

- ◆ The Russell 2000 is made up of 2,000 smaller companies with a median size of about $400 million.
- ◆ The MSCI EAFE stands for the Morgan Stanley Capital International Europe, Australasia and Far East Index, which tracks foreign companies located in 21 developed nations, among them Great Britain, Japan, Germany, France, and Singapore. It provides a quick check to see how overseas holdings are doing.

All of the stocks within these indexes are in various stages of development. For example, the largest-capitalization stocks on the New York Stock Exchange recently included the familiar names GE, Coca-Cola, Exxon, Merck, Philip Morris, Procter & Gamble, IBM, Bristol-Myers Squibb, Pfizer, and Johnson & Johnson. Some pundits believe their time has passed, while others are convinced they'll shine on Nasdaq downturns. Deciding stocks, old or new, are ripe for the picking requires some patience to avoid moving too quickly or too slowly. Examine each stock individually in the context of its peers. In the words of a well-known wine commercial: "We sell no wine before its time." If only investors could be so patient and confident.

22
LEGAL TENDER
COMES IN HANDY

"The lack of money is the root of all evil."

While Mark Twain didn't build his world around money, he did consider it quite helpful in living comfortably. At one point, he lived in Europe for a decade in order to reduce his family's cost of living. As singer Pearl Bailey once put it: "I've been rich and I've been poor, and rich is better." Twain's philosophical assessment of wealth has clear parallels to today, though the actual forms of money underwent significant change during his lifetime. The U.S. government issued its first paper money in 1862, called greenbacks because their green ink made them different from gold certificates. The first U.S. coin with the portrait of a president on it was the 1909 Abraham Lincoln penny, a coin which today many people don't stoop to pick up on the sidewalk.

Our currency continues to undergo change in modern times:

+ In 1969, bills over $100 in value were discontinued because there was little demand for them, thereby removing McKinley, Cleveland, Madison, Chase, and Wilson.

+ The Susan B. Anthony dollar coin never became popular, nor did the Thomas Jefferson $2 bill.

+ A major redesign of U.S. currency to thwart counterfeiters began in 1996, first with the $100 bill and followed by subsequent bills. The big, off-center pictures still look odd to a lot of folks.

Because the dollar remains important, investors should keep an eye on monetary policy. The Federal Reserve System continues to have high visibility as the national bank that oversees the nation's monetary policies. Its role is to maintain the value of the dollar and keep our economy healthy. The Fed's Open Market Committee, for example, makes decisions on short-term interest rates, which has tremendous impact on the spending and borrowing patterns of Americans. The comments of the Fed chairman are often the most closely-followed of any government official because the Fed's moves can have a dramatic impact on the cost of buying a house, using credit cards, or financing a car. In addition, boosting interest rates makes fixed-rate investment such as bonds more attractive and often drives investors out of stocks. One word from the Fed chairman can send the stock market into tumult. All of this underscores the simple fact that the buck stops at the Fed.

Whatever physical form money may take, following it has become one of the most active national pastimes. From the *Wall Street Journal* to CNBC financial cable television, from investment newsletters to Internet financial sites, there are countless venues for learning how to amass more money or track the progress of the money one already has. In the twenty-first century of escalating home and general living costs, being without money is deemed an evil. Not understanding how money works may be an even greater sin because of the negative impact on yourself and your family. Twain traveled extensively and lived well; money made it possible.

AMERICAN HUMOUR.

From lecture brochure making reference to the short story,
"The Celebrated Jumping Frog of Calaveras County."

23

USE NEW TECHNOLOGY AS A TOOL

"The early machine was full of caprices, full of defects—devilish ones. It had as many immoralities as the machine of today has virtues."

(on using an early typewriter)

In its early history, the typewriter was indeed daunting, in much the same way the Internet is today. Frustration is often a byproduct of progress, even for an inventor and forward thinker like Mark Twain. The Internet provides great information on being a smart investor—so long as you are patient and learn how to sift through that cornucopia of ideas. If you don't go about your searches in a somewhat organized fashion, you will simply see "stuff" about investments fly by and be none the wiser. You must always consider where the information is coming from and determine the credibility of the source. That mastered, you have at your fingertips data and advice that investors a generation ago could only dream about and which only top professional investors were able to tap.

You'll find some familiar names and faces on Internet investment sites that provide a common sense approach to sorting out your finances. For example, The Motley Fool, featuring the advice of the jester-capped brothers David and Tom Gardner, features the same sense of whimsy in its online *www.fool.com* site that it exhibits in its popular investment books, columns, and on-air reports. Twain, of course, would have appreciated its non-broker-like personality. Meanwhile, Intuit, long dominant in sales of tax software through its Quicken product, provides an array of tax and personal finance information on its *www.quicken.com* site that draws in customers who have previously used its products during tax season. Of course, we know that Twain figured anything that could slow the progress of the tax man was worthwhile. Do you follow your mutual funds through various Morningstar Mutual Funds publications and software? With *www.morningstar.com,* you'll find columns and up-to-date comparative information on stocks and annuities as well as funds.

Financial web sites include those that are extensions of existing print publications, television networks, or software products; those presenting a specific investment philosophy; and others that primarily provide financial data and tracking information. You'll find that financial web sites are incredibly incestuous, in that many carry news and features from other web services as well as their own. Many sites charge fees for analyst reports or other aspects of what they consider to be premium service.

Here are the best ways to choose among investment Internet sites:

◆ Follow each site you're interested in for a full week to see whether you're getting the full information you need to make your decisions. See if any of the columnists or features are especially useful or entertaining, and whether you want to continue to follow them.

◆ Are the links to additional information on the site useful or outdated? Sometimes a web site's home page may look comparable to those of the competition, but its backup information is sparse. Track a stock, mutual fund, or investment topic through the site to see how it is covered.

◆ Go over the unique features that a site offers. It may, for example, include an archive of past articles from your favorite financial periodical or excellent do-it-yourself computations of how taxes will impact your personal investment results.

◆ If you seek daily information such as stock quotes or need access to trading, see which site makes this available effortlessly and understandably. Some of this information you may already receive from your discount or online broker, making an additional web site unnecessary.

Among web sites tied to popular publications, TV, or software are: CBS Marketwatch (*www.cbs.marketwatch.com*); CNBC (*www.cnbc.com*); CNNFn (*www.cnnfn.com*); *Wall Street Journal* (*www.interactive.wsj.com*); *Microsoft Investor* (*www. moneycentral.msn.com*); *Money* Magazine (*www.money.com*); *Worth* Magazine (*www.worth.com*); and *Kiplinger's* Magazine (*www.kiplinger.com*).

There are many sites with ties to personalities and specialized presentation such as TheStreet.com (*www.thestreet.com*)

that's best-known for high-profile stock maven James Cramer; and Brill's Mutual Funds Interactive (*www.brill.com*) that builds on the reputation of fund pundit Marla Brill. For investors seeking sophisticated trading assistance and information, there's the Thomson Investors Network (*www.thomsoninvest.net*); DBC Online (*www.dbc.com*); Quote.com (*www.quote.com*); ZD Interactive Investor (*www.zdii.com*); Briefing.com (*www.briefing.com*); and Reuters MoneyNet.com (*www.moneynet.com*).

These sites are just the tip of the iceberg. There are many, many others that deal with more specialized needs, whether you are researching 401(k) plans or searching for quality collectibles. The only way to find whether one works for you is to put it through its paces several times. If you aren't satisfied, move on to another site, just as Twain moved on to a better-working typewriter.

24
MONEY CHANGES EVERYTHING

"Make money and the whole world will conspire to call you a gentleman."

Respected both in his time and after his time, Mark Twain received more than his share of honors. Yet he employed self-effacing humor to keep from getting carried away by it all. "To be made a master of arts by your venerable college is an event of large size to me," he wrote in a letter accepting an honorary degree from Yale, "and a distinction which gratifies me quite as much as if I deserved it." Similarly, though he greatly admired many aspects of the progress of the modern industrialized world, he loved to prick the balloon of inflated business egos. He believed that the same individual with identical personality and manners, should he strike it rich, is given far greater respect and admiration by society than the similar, but poorer specimen.

Today, the vast number of university buildings and hospital wings bearing the names of the rich is admirable in terms of what is ultimately accomplished for the good of mankind. Nonetheless, the likes of Michael Milken and Ivan Boesky were similarly feted for their generous contributions to universities and various charitable causes prior to their being convicted of illegal market manipulation. Money can often cloud a critical eye.

"Vast wealth, to the person unaccustomed to it, is a bane; it eats into the flesh and bone of his morals," Twain wrote in "The $30,000 Bequest." Today our society is diligent in trying to find the sparkling, admirable aspects within those who have become wealthy. Someone who would be considered dull, dull, dull becomes intriguing because a hard-working, intuitive nature paid off. This could describe the youthful heads of software or Internet companies who became fabulously wealthy in their twenties, the chief executive officers who climbed the corporate ladder, the shrewd traders who made a fortune in the market, or the aspiring film students who made it big on the silver screen. Thanks to money, their ticket is now punched for entry into the finest clubs, the best restaurants, select parties, and the celebrity watch.

Twain once told a newspaper reporter, "To succeed in business, avoid my example." Yet he was the successful inventor of "Mark Twain's Patent Self-Pasting Scrap Book," which featured strips of glue on pages that users could dampen, and came in 30 sizes and models. This invention made more money for him than his books in the year it was introduced. Unfortunately, he lost more than half a million dollars in other innovations in which he invested over the years, such as a typesetter, an overwhelmingly-complicated board game that only he could play, and even a nutritional supplement. Yet his notebooks are full of many ideas that were well ahead of their time, such as microfilm and a television-like machine that used "pictures transferred by light." His novel *Pudd'nhead Wilson* included fingerprinting as a primary plot component that drew the entire story together, even though the process hadn't yet been introduced.

It was in business ventures, such as publishing, that Twain had his financial ups and downs. In an era before self-help books offered easy steps to becoming a millionaire, he always picked himself up, even if it meant moving to Europe. He put his mind to work and proceeded to the next adventure. Twain died a wealthy man. Coupled with careful financial planning, it was what he did best—his writing and lecturing—that made him one.

THE AUTHOR'S MEMORIES.

The narrator at work on *A Tramp Abroad*
as depicted in the book's frontispiece.

25
DAYS OF RISK MEAN
NIGHTS OF ANGUISH

"There are two times in a man's life when he should not speculate: when he can afford it, and when he can't."

(Following the Equator)

Every era has its "walk on the wild side." In Mark Twain's youth, it was prospecting for precious metals in the wild, wild west. His adventures took place in the Nevada Territory, where his brother Orion Clemens had been appointed secretary. Twain, a youthful unofficial secretary to the secretary, came west in a horse-drawn coach. His first venture was a less-than-successful foray into the lumber industry, in which he accidentally set fire to the small forest that was on his claim. It burned to the ground.

Then his fledgling Clemens Gold and Silver Mining Company bought mining claims bearing names such as the Sam Patch Lode, Horatio Lode, and the Magna Charta Ledge, the miners digging day and night with pick and shovel for fortunes that alas were never unearthed. Besides the back-breaking hard work, there were hard facts of life in this unique form of speculation: The assayer's report on a claim was usually based on the richest fragment of ore, not a representative sample, and even the most promising claims generally proved to be completely worthless.

Today's daredevils chase after profits trading stocks, and are known as *day traders*. It is a wild, wild occupation. Day traders, by definition, open and close their positions in the same day, jumping in as soon as they have a sense of the day's action. The average length of time that a day trader holds a position is a scant seven minutes, involving about 700 shares. The excitement is the good news; the result is the bad news. Regulators estimate that no more than 10 percent of day traders actually make any money. The Electronic Traders Association, an industry trade group, maintains more optimistically that one-third turn a profit, another one-third stay about even, and the rest lose money. All the hot trading activity isn't spread around either: Three percent of day traders account for 60 percent of their volume. Day traders as a group now account for more than 25 percent of the volume on the Nasdaq stock market. Such traders claim that they make the market much more efficient, while critics contend that they contribute to its volatility. Unlike someone trading through most online brokers, a system in which an order goes to a wholesaler who then fills it, professional day traders trade their own accounts. That makes it possible to take advantage of sophisticated computer tools that include direct access to private electronic computerized networks.

One day-trading strategy tries to buy on the bid (the price a prospective buyer is willing to pay for a stock) and immediately sell on the ask (the lowest price acceptable to a prospective seller of the same security), using the ability to execute split-second trades to turn an immediate profit. Other strategies attempt to take advantage of volatile stocks, buying on dips, and selling minutes later when momentum resumes. Some day traders are risk-takers working from home, others are former Wall Street pros with unlimited resources, and the remainder are semi-pros working out of day-trading shops. Traders scan news reports, fundamentals, technical analysis, newsletters, chat rooms, and Nasdaq trading data to plot their moves. The two elements of day-trading success are a good decision support system that tells you when to buy and sell, and a good grasp of mechanics involved in trade execution. If you don't view day trading as a "career path," forget about it. Frequent trading is expensive even at online rates, it's difficult to move as fast as real professional traders, you must always cover your losses, and you can be whacked by computer breakdowns.

Those making less than five trades a day should stick to the Internet rather than working through a day-trading firm. For example, someone starting with $100,000 must be prepared to lose $30,000 to $50,000 as part of the learning curve the first six months. Day trading makes the most sense for someone "in transition" between jobs or with time to spend at home, not someone intending to quit a stable job in order to get started. The best way is to "practice" first without actually trading. Then begin with lower-priced, less volatile stocks to test theories with as little risk as possible and control your losses. Prospective day traders are often not told the risks or difficulty. They often don't understand they'll be independent contractors without the typical protections investors have. Day trading is the modern opportunity to cast your fate to the wind. If you think it's for you, hold on tight for the ride.

JIM STANDING A SIEGE.

Tom Sawyer Abroad

26

YOU MUST GIVE THE TAX MAN HIS DUE

"What is the difference between a taxidermist and a tax collector? Answer: A taxidermist takes only your skin."

Death and taxes are still as inevitable as they were in Mark Twain's day. It was during his lifetime that income taxes in particular became a hot subject. The first income taxes were imposed by the U.S. government to pay for the Civil War, but then repealed in 1872. A 2 percent income tax on personal income over $4,000 was enacted in 1894, but rejected as unconstitutional by the U.S. Supreme Court. (Where are those justices now when we need them?) A constitutional amendment was proposed to permit a personal income tax in 1909; it became law in 1913, and income taxes have been collected ever since. While there are now more taxes and they are infinitely more complicated, there are also numerous tax aids to help you out.

The days of purely shoebox recordkeeping are numbered, as technology has become the taxpayer's friend. The key is to be organized and not rely too much on memory. With tax software, online information, and electronic filing now readily available, you can take advantage of new efficiencies. Put your expenses on a computer program to make your information more reliable. File your receipts where you can find them. In particular, use technology to file early if you're due a refund. Electronic tax filing reduces errors, ensures that the IRS received your return, and gets you your refund in record time. If you received a large refund on your last tax filing, you should probably adjust your withholding at work. After all, why give Uncle Sam a free loan? In terms of income, the withholding tables aren't adequate unless you have a considerable number of itemized deductions. Marriage, a new home, or a new baby can also dictate filling out a new W-4 form. Make a careful tax decision on how many exemptions you should claim. If you are self-employed, figure out what your estimated quarterly payments should be early in the year. Keep track of income to make sure you're on schedule throughout the year.

Here are some additional steps to trim your tax bill:

+ Contribute the maximum to accounts such as company 401(k) retirement plans. If you haven't been contributing the maximum, some companies let you catch up with a late contribution for the current year.

+ Self-employed individuals should set up their Keogh plans by Dec. 31, though they can contribute up until the tax-filing deadline. Choose between a conventional individual retirement account in which you must pay tax

when withdrawing upon retirement, versus a nonde-
ductible Roth IRA that lets you forego the eventual tax
bite when you withdraw. (Remember that the income
ceiling on the Roth IRA is $150,000 for married couples
and $95,000 for single people.)

+ Always contribute to your IRA early in the tax year so that
your money is put to work as soon as possible, since even
a few months each year can have a dramatic impact on
your eventual payout.

In other areas, carefully record mileage for business in a
book kept in your car. If you're thinking of a tax-deductible
charitable contribution, donate appreciated stock or property,
and avoid paying capital gains. It could take time to transfer the
stock or property. Get a receipt or written acknowledgment of
any type of donation you make. If you claim your contribution's value at less than $500, there's no extra paperwork. If you
value it at $500 or more, you must complete Section A of Form
8283 and make sure the IRS has certified the recipient as a qual-
ifying organization.

Additional tax-saving steps involve making tax-free gifts
to children and grandchildren and investing in tax-free municipal bonds. Though you should consult a tax professional about
major decisions regarding your taxes, the basics of getting
organized are still up to you. Careful planning can leave you
happier each April and reduce the chances of the IRS "taking
your skin."

"COURTING ON THE SLY."

Adventures of Huckleberry Finn

27
MONEY CAN'T BUY YOU LOVE

"How my heart goes out in sympathy to you! How I do pity you, Commodore Vanderbilt! Most men have at least a few friends, whose devotion is a comfort and a solace to them, but you seem to be the idol of only a crawling swarm of small souls, who love to glorify your most flagrant unworthiness in print; or praise your vast possessions worshippingly; or sing of your unimportant private habits and sayings and doings, as if your millions gave them dignity; friends who applaud your superhuman stinginess with the same gusto that they do your most magnificent displays of commercial genius and daring, and likewise your most lawless violations of commercial honor—for those infatuated worshippers of dollars not their own seem to make no distinction, but swing their hats and shout hallelujah every time you do anything, no matter what it is."

("Open Letter to Commodore Vanderbilt")

Railroad and steamship tycoon Cornelius Vanderbilt, despite his incredible business acumen, symbolized to Mark Twain pure greed and a complete lack of conscience. Beginning with a Staten Island ferry service he started as a teenager, the ambitious Vanderbilt expanded into steamship routes during the California Gold Rush and later became head of the New York Central Railroad. He was one of America's richest men, a distinction he passed on to his son and grandson. Twain's comments to the Commodore appeared in a *Packard's Monthly* article. Annoyed that praise was heaped upon Vanderbilt strictly due to his enormous wealth, Twain believed that his ruthlessness and stinginess made him unworthy.

The very wealthy are both revered and berated these days:

◆ There are several Internet sites devoted entirely to regularly tracking Microsoft Chairman Bill Gates' personal wealth, which exceeds $100 billion by some counts. The richest American—Gates—could, according to one estimate, give $275 to each and every person in the United States (an act unlikely to occur).

◆ In the entertainment field, *Star Wars* creator George Lucas earned $400 million in 1999, a 50 percent gain over the prior year's winner, television comedian Jerry Seinfeld. These figures are recounted with both awe and envy, since the public nature of stock holdings and entertainment box office results make it much easier to estimate personal wealth than it was in Twain's day.

◆ Rather than avoid positive causes, business stars donate considerable money to charitable causes as a matter of course and tax laws make such contributions even more attractive.

◆ Though some may criticize the power that techno-leaders wield, a goal of many young Americans joining the "dot-com" workplace is to get stock options, enjoy an initial public offering, and, hopefully, become very rich.

Twain certainly did not worship the vast possessions of Vanderbilt or express fascination with his personal habits, as he felt many other Americans did. Brains and hard work are often major factors in attaining wealth, but another factor, luck, often plays an even bigger role. Having great wealth doesn't necessarily give you a riveting personality or a story to tell, but it does assure that some folks will be curious about how much you have and how your life is different from theirs because of all those greenbacks. Don't expect to receive many "hallelujahs," however. Those days are long gone.

A more upbeat exchange, a Twain letter to Andrew Carnegie and the industrialist/philanthropist's response, follows:

"Dear Sir and Friend,

You seem to be in prosperity. Could you lend an admirer $1.50 to buy a hymn-book with? I will bless you. God will bless you—I feel it; I know it—and it will do a great deal of good.

Yours truly,

Mark Twain

P.S. Don't send the hymn-book; send the money. I want to make the selection myself."

A good-natured Carnegie wrote back in reply: "Nothing less than a two-dollar and a half hymn-book gilt will do for you. Your place in the choir (celestial) demands that and you shall have it."

SELLING A MINE.

Roughing It

28
LEAVE A MARGIN
FOR ERROR

"One day, back in the Sixties when I was living in San
Francisco, I got a tip from Mr. Camp, a bold man who
was always making big fortunes in ingenious specu-
lations and losing them again in the course of six
months by other speculative ingenuities. Camp told
me to buy some shares in the Hale and Norcross
(mining company). I bought fifty shares at three hundred dollars a share. I bought on a margin and put up
20 per cent. It exhausted my funds. I wrote Orion
(Twain's older brother) and offered him half and
asked him to send his share of the money. I waited
and waited. He wrote and said he was going to
attend to it. The stock went along up pretty briskly. It
went higher and higher. It reached a thousand dollars
a share. It climbed to two thousand, then to three
thousand; then to twice that figure. The money did
not come but I was not disturbed. By and by that
stock took a turn and began to gallop down. Then I
wrote urgently. Orion answered that he had sent the
money long ago—said he had sent to the Occidental
Hotel. I inquired for it. They said it was not there. To
cut a long story short, that stock went on down until

it fell below the price I paid for it. Then it began to eat up the margin, and when at last I got out I was very badly crippled.

"When it was too late I found out what had become of Orion's money. Any other human being would have sent a check but he sent gold. The hotel clerk put it in the safe and never thought of it again, and there it reposed all this time, enjoying its fatal work, no doubt. Another man might have thought to tell me that the money was not in a letter but was in an express package, but it never occurred to Orion to do that."

(The Autobiography of Mark Twain)

The margin account is a tricky critter today, just as it was when it cleaned out the young Mark Twain's bank account after his older brother Orion didn't get him his money to meet a margin call in a timely fashion. Modern investors betting heavily on technology stocks with borrowed money have similarly paid the price during sudden Nasdaq market downturns in the new century. The positive side to a margin account is that it can help you increase the potential return on your stock investment by permitting you to borrow money from your brokerage firm to make an initial purchase of securities. Basically, the broker asks for securities or cash as collateral and you can usually borrow up to 50 percent of the value of your common stocks, mutual funds, and corporate bonds. You can also borrow up to 90 percent of the value of Treasury securities. If you can sell the stock at a higher price than you paid, you repay the loan, plus interest and commission, and enjoy your profit.

Sounds great. But there's a reason why margin buying was a high-risk factor contributing to the Crash of 1929. If the stock drops in value, as it did in Twain's case and for many investors in 1929, 1987, and in more recent declines, you still have to repay the loan. If you must sell the shares for less than you paid, your losses could be greater than if you'd owned the stock outright. In a precipitous market drop, panic over losses can quickly set in for heavily-margined investors.

In light of the dangers following major stock crashes, regulatory rules require that you must maintain a margin balance of cash or securities equaling at least 25 percent of the total market value of the securities in the account at all times. Most firms, however, have higher maintenance requirements, which are typically between 30 and 40 percent of the market value.

Know the process beforehand when buying stock on margin:

+ To open a margin account, you must deposit a minimum of $2,000 in cash or eligible securities. All margin trades must be conducted through that account.

+ If the market value of your investment falls below the required limit, the brokerage firm issues a margin call.

+ You must meet the call by adding money to your account to bring it to the required minimum, or sell the stock, pay back your broker and take the loss.

+ Let's say, for example, that shares worth $16,000 were purchased by borrowing $8,000. The market value of the securities subsequently dropped to $12,000 and, as a result, the equity in the account fell to $4,000. If your firm has a maintenance requirement of 40 percent, you'll have to add $800 to bring your margin account up to $4,800.

The average investor should not be heavily margined, due to the potential downside. It is perfectly fine to buy a portion of your investments on margin, however, so long as you realize that the potential rewards also carry significant risk. Being aggressive with some of your money can result in growth for your portfolio. But you obviously don't want to be "badly crippled" as Twain was.

29
CONSIDER THE WORLD YOUR INVESTMENT OYSTER

> "The gentle reader will never, never know what a consummate ass he can become until he goes abroad."
>
> *(Innocents Abroad)*

Mark Twain was a world traveler, writing travel books and articles, even living abroad with his family for a decade. In *The Prince and the Pauper* and *A Connecticut Yankee in King Arthur's Court* he challenged the inequities and hypocrisy of the European social system, just as he had taken America to task. His writing was popular in England, where he was awarded an honorary degree from Oxford. He was a sophisticated internationalist in favor of fewer barriers between nations. "I don't know of a single foreign product that enters this country untaxed except the answer to prayer," he once complained.

In the twenty-first century, many barriers between nations are down. But it is in the area of investments where one of the final roadblocks is being removed. It's true that the

United States still holds nearly half of the total market capitalization worldwide, but that percentage has been eroding for two decades. The United Kingdom has a market capitalization of about 10 percent, followed closely by Japan with about a half-percentage-point less. Germany, France, and Switzerland have about 4 percent apiece, while the Netherlands holds nearly 3 percent. The world's most blistering performance in recent years has been turned in by little Finland (which boasts the powerhouse cell phone maker Nokia), followed by Spain and Belgium. The U.S. came next, followed by Greece, the Netherlands, Ireland, Sweden, Switzerland, and Italy. Europe has been hit by the same wave of mergers and initial public offerings that transformed the U.S. market.

American investors have increasingly been adding foreign stocks to their personal portfolios, mostly through mutual funds or American Depositary Receipts (ADRs), which represent foreign stocks traded on U.S. exchanges. As the interest in global investing has accelerated, U.S. brokerage firms have rapidly expanded their research presence to meet the demand. The argument is made that this is a sensible diversification move. However, daily economic events seem to affect all world markets to some degree, so many investors wonder whether international investing is as much of a diversification move as it was in the past. The answer is that there's not as much correlation between the markets as you might think. On a given day when the U.S. markets decline, that event is often followed by declines in Asia and Europe. However, if you study any period over the past 40 years, you'll see little connection. For example, the U.S. market enjoyed a bull run at the same time the Tokyo stock market was in the dumpster. Recent world stock market results also indicate that markets do have minds of their own.

There are many quality foreign stocks to choose from. Other than some of the obvious consumer names such as Japan's Honda Motor Company (ticker symbol HMC as an ADR trading here) or Sony Corporation (SNE), there are many foreign firms that provide products or services you're familiar with even if you didn't know the parent firm. For example, the U.K.'s Diageo Plc. (DEO) owns Burger King and Guinness; Switzerland's Novartis A.G. (NVTSY) makes antacid Maalox and athlete's foot treatment Desenex; and Japan's Ito-Yokado Company (IYCOY) operates thousands of 7-Eleven stores in the U.S. France's AXA S.A. (AXA) owns 60 percent of AXA Financial (formerly the Equitable Companies) and 73 percent of the Donaldson, Lufkin & Jenrette investment bank. Fujitsu Limited (FJTSY) owns Japan's comprehensive online service provider; Luxembourg's Quilmes Industrial S.A. (LQU) is a leader in Latin American beer markets; and Hong Kong-based Hutchison Whampoa Limited (HUWHY) is an enormous conglomerate whose largest shareholder is one of the world's wealthiest men.

Here's what you should keep in mind as you invest internationally:

+ Your first step should probably be a diversified mutual fund investing in the stocks of many countries, shifting its assets around as world conditions change. Don't pick a region or a single country investment, since the chance of volatility is far greater.

+ Realize that companies trading as ADRs on major exchanges here have agreed to meet the accounting standards of the U.S. and those exchanges. Their information is therefore more extensive than so-called "pink sheet" ADRs that don't meet those stringent requirements. They can be compared directly to U.S. companies so that you're comparing "apples to apples."

✦ Whenever you invest in the equities of another country, your stock is subject to political change and currency fluctuations in addition to the regular uncertainties of investment. These extra components require that you monitor your holdings closely.

✦ Popular foreign firms usually have their own web sites in English that give you the opportunity to learn more about them.

Don't become overwrought with the world's cares as you expand your horizons. As Twain noted in an interview in a New York newspaper:

> "I couldn't get any fun out of England. It is too grave a country. And its gravity soaks into the stranger and makes him as serious as everybody else. When I was there I couldn't seem to think of anything but deep problems of government, taxes, free trade, finance—and every night I went to bed drunk with statistics."

The top-performing diversified international stock funds in annualized return over the five years ending with the first quarter of 2000, according to Morningstar Mutual Funds, were:

✦ Pilgrim International Small Cap Growth Portfolio—Class A; $2,000 minimum initial investment; 5.75 percent front-end "load"; 800-334-3444; annualized return 37 percent.

+ American Century International Discovery Fund—
  Investor Class; $10,000 minimum initial investment; no-
  load; 800-345-2021; five-year annualized return 37 percent.

+ Janus Overseas Fund; temporarily closed to new investment at time of publication; 800-525-8983; annualized
  return 36 percent.

+ Concert Investment International Equity Fund—Class A;
  $250 minimum; 5.5 percent load, 800-344-5445; annual-
  ized return 36 percent.

+ T. Rowe Price International Discovery Fund; $2,500
  minimum; no-load; 800-638-5660; annualized return 31
  percent.

his

Waw—ho — no—fah

mark

SATISFACTORY VOUCHER.

Roughing It

30

DON'T LET DEBT SEND YOU UP THE RIVER

"The fact that man invented imprisonment for debt, proves that man is an idiot & also that he is utterly vile & malignant. How can imprisonment pay a debt? Was the idea of it to pay the creditor in revenge?"

Income tax evasion was the one offense on which the government was able to get Chicago mobster Al Capone convicted and finally sent to prison. In that instance, imprisonment was a useful alternative. But, in general, the concept of debtors prison has fallen from favor for the very reason Mark Twain points out here: You can't draw water from a stone. Most creditors would rather work out a plan to get paid back their money than seek retribution. These days the IRS is showing some heart by auditing fewer than 1 percent of all individual income-tax returns—down considerably from the past—due to tight budgeting, reduced staffing, and efforts to improve service.

Still, minding your P's and Q's can help you avoid penalties and keep you from being sent up the river. It pays to be timely, because the Internal Revenue Service will hit you with interest and penalties if you don't file your tax return or pay taxes that you owe by their due date.

Here's why you shouldn't pay the taxes you owe late:

- ✦ Even if a filing extension has been granted, the IRS will charge you interest on late taxes. In recent years, that interest charge has fluctuated between 8 and 10 percent.
- ✦ There's an interest charge on the penalties imposed for failure to file a return, too (in addition to any penalties imposed for negligence or fraud).
- ✦ The interest is charged on the penalty from the return's due date, including extensions.
- ✦ When you pay taxes late, the penalty is generally 0.5 percent of the unpaid amount for each month or part of a month the tax isn't paid. The penalty can't exceed 25 percent of the unpaid amount and applies to any unpaid tax on the return.

There's more to worry about if you file your return late (including extensions):

- ✦ The penalty is usually 5 percent of the amount for each month or part of a month your return is late, unless you have a reasonable explanation.
- ✦ If you attach your explanation to the return, you might not be charged with the penalty.
- ✦ If your return is more than 60 days late, the minimum penalty will be $100 or the amount of any tax you owe, whichever is smaller.

Meanwhile, if you make estimated tax payments, any penalty is assessed from the installment due date to the date paid or the original due date of the return, whichever is earlier. The rate of the penalty is the same as the rate of interest for underpayments of tax. However, the penalty is not compounded daily, while the interest is.

The bottom line remains: Pay your taxes on time. It's burdensome enough to be shelling money out to Uncle Sam without building up an even bigger bill because you didn't do it in a timely fashion. Tax filing behind you, you'll be able to spend more time trying to minimize your taxes by itemizing, contributing to retirement accounts, timing bonus payments, and making charitable contributions. Rest assured that Mark Twain would approve of any steps taken to avoid the hated tax man.

"DOFF THY RAGS AND DON THESE SPLENDORS."

The Prince and the Pauper

31
ENJOY LIFE, BUT NOT ON THE CHEAP

> "I would rather live on $100 a month and live like a human being, than have $8 more and live like an owl."

While his origins were humble, Mark Twain knew how to live well. "Recently some one in Missouri has sent me a picture of the house I was born in," he once wrote. "Heretofore I have always stated that it was a palace, but I shall be more guarded, now." He understood the difference between being frugal and being downright cheap. After all, what good is money if you don't enjoy a comfortable life? Twain and his family traveled extensively, he always dressed fashionably, and they lived well here and abroad. His last home, an 18-room Italian-style villa near Redding, Connecticut, was designed and constructed with his sparse instructions that it have rooms big enough for his billiard table and orchastrelle (an instrument like an organ) and that he didn't have to visit it until the day he actually

moved in. It was called Stormfield because the $60,000 in prof-
its from the sale of his story "Captain Stormfield's Visit to
Heaven" helped pay to finish it in 1908. It featured electric
lights and a steam generator for heat. Comfort was always king
for Twain: He often did his writing in bed, especially in his later
years, remaining ensconced there even when visitors arrived.
He also loved fine cigars.

Today's preoccupation with the good life on a budget is
strong, exemplified by the success of Martha Stewart's tasteful
life "accents" and the popularity of a myriad of guides such as
Consumer Reports that help people buy everything from cars to
cell phones to vacuum cleaners. Enjoying the good life on a
budget requires careful planning, but each and every weekend
American families fan out to discount stores and garage sales to
snap up goodies at bargain prices. Just be sure your needs correlate to what you buy and that you bargain carefully.

Keeping in mind Twain's observation from *The Gilded Age*
that "A man pretty much always refuses another man's first offer,
no matter what it is," follow these tips for getting the best deal:

+ Do your own research, be willing to accept highly-rated
  products that may not necessarily be the most chic, and use
  the Internet and catalogs to comparison-shop effectively.

+ As your grandmother may have already instructed you,
  sometimes it makes sense to buy a brand name because
  the quality is higher, while in other cases you're doing
  nothing more than just showing off.

+ Avoid extended warranties or fancy financing deals, watch
  out for "bait and switch" advertising, save your receipts,
  and be aware of the return policy before you buy anything.

- ◆ If you're into garage sales, spend some time learning about the types of items you may be interested in, try to think logically about what you need to buy, and avoid getting bowled over by impulse.

- ◆ When shopping for a car, be a hard-nosed negotiator. Whether buying or leasing, get all the specifics and fine print spelled out for you before you ever get serious. Demand to be told each and every cost you'll encounter before you drive the vehicle away. Once again, your flexibility in selection of that vehicle could save you big bucks. Don't expect too many deals on the very hottest models.

Your deal-making can result in a better lifestyle. Plan to leave a financial legacy for your heirs, but don't "live like an owl" to do it. Everyone always gets a kick out of a motor home or fancy car with the bumper sticker "Our Children's Inheritance." If you play your financial cards right, you can enjoy life and the kids will be well taken care of, too.

A NEW MINE.

Roughing It

32
THERE'S STILL ONE BORN EVERY MINUTE

> "We needed three dollars and did not know where to get it. While we were in a quandary I espied a valuable dog on the street. I picked up the canine and sold him to a man for three dollars. Afterward the owner of the dog came along and I got three dollars from him for telling him where the dog was. So I went back and gave the three dollars to the man whom I sold it to, and I have lived honestly ever since."

W ell, the man did get his dog back, didn't he? Rest assured, Mark Twain did not actually commit this scam that allegedly netted three dollars, but he was aware of the gullibility of the average citizen and the ever-present opportunities to make a buck from a "white lie." Flim-flam was common back then and still is today. For example, Ponzi schemes, one of the oldest examples of fraud, are still with us. Though named for Charles Ponzi, a 1920s scoundrel, they were around in Twain's time. Such pyramid scams promise tremendous investment returns from precious metals, real estate, or the selling of products. The early investors are paid off with the money that comes from people who are taken in by the scheme later. Once the onslaught of new victims slows down, the money evaporates, and the Ponzi collapses. The Ponzi artist skips town with a lot of other people's money.

The film *Boiler Room* released in 2000 chronicled another very common scam: A group of salespeople work out of a cramped office with a bank of telephones, employing smooth talk about unbelievable profits, no risk, and the need to act immediately. Such operations play upon an individual's greed. They fleece many a gullible investor, taking money for often nonexistent investments, and then leave town when the authorities get wind of their game. They did the same sting in Twain's time, minus the telephone. And, of course, the newest game plan involves bogus deals sent out over the Internet. Same basic idea, different periods of history.

Whenever anyone pitches an investment idea to you:

+ Always request information in writing, and take time to analyze it.

+ Show it to others to get their opinions. Don't naively send your money too quickly.

+ As always, a deal that sounds too good to be true probably is.

Among other investments to be wary about are limited partnerships loaded with big commissions, expenses, and fees. These may involve oil and gas, equipment leasing, or real estate and often have a minimum investment of $5,000. Once you're in, forget about getting out because aftermarket for bad deals isn't all that strong. You could lose your shirt. Your investment is in the hands of the general partner and you have no say in how it's run. Sometimes claims are made that these offer big tax advantages, but in reality even that is merely a pipe dream.

Precious metals such as gold, silver, and platinum are another area in which fast-talk artists promise skyrocketing price gains that have no ties to reality. If underlying prices have increased, the pitch is that they'll increase even more in the future. If prices are down, the pitch is that they're about to rebound. You have a 50/50 chance, just as in Twain's lifetime. "In our late canvas half of the nation believed that in silver lay salvation, the other half as passionately believed that way lay destruction," Twain wrote in his essay "Corne-Pone Opinions." "Do you believe that a tenth part of the people, on either side, had any rational excuse for having an opinion about the matter at all? I studied that mighty question to the bottom—and came out empty."

Mark Twain's tale about a dog was fun, just as the old Paul Newman/Robert Redford movie *The Sting* that set up a fake horse-racing betting parlor was fun. But if you become a victim of a Ponzi scheme, a flawed limited partnership, or wind up holding a lot of devalued metal, the joke unfortunately will be on you.

INCIPIENT MILLIONAIRES.

Roughing It

33

PILOT YOUR FINANCIAL COURSE EARLY

> "When I was twenty-seven years old, I was a mining broker's clerk in San Francisco, and an expert in all the details of stock traffic. I was alone in the world, and had nothing to depend upon but my wits and a clean reputation; but these were setting my feet in the road to eventual fortune, and I was content with the prospect."
>
> *("The 1,000,000 Pound Bank-Note")*

Some say youth is wasted on the young, but many young people do use it quite wisely. Stop and smell the roses as you enjoy early adult life, but also improve your investment knowledge and portfolio. Like the mining broker's clerk, you could be on "the road to eventual fortune." In his own youth, Mark Twain enjoyed four years as a riverboat pilot on the Mississippi before all peaceful traffic was ended by the Civil War. It was a heady time before the railroads nudged the riverboats aside.

To get started in this prestigious profession, he had to pay $100 in cash and $400 to be paid out of his first earnings after receiving his license. But he would eventually make more than $150 a month, noting that two month's salary "would pay a preacher's salary for a year" and included free room and board. The pilot, he noted, "comes at no man's beck or call, obeys no man's orders, & scorns all men's suggestions." In *Life on the Mississippi,* he also learned in his training as a cub pilot that water levels and weather conditions could make the job especially demanding: "Two things became pretty apparent to me. One was, that in order to be a pilot a man had to learn more than any one man ought to be allowed to know; and the other was, that he must learn it all over again in a different way every twenty-four hours."

Use your twenties as a time to establish a good credit record, to develop a habit of saving 10 percent or more of your income, and to pay off any education-related debt you may have incurred. Make sure you always have sufficient, ongoing insurance coverage. Don't throw every extra cent into buying a fancy car or entertainment equipment, but instead start gradually building your savings with the goal of owning a home one day. You're a part of an exciting new period of self-determination for investors, with the help of electronic trading, the Internet, discount fees, and more information on investing your money than ever before.

Unlike your parents' generation, throughout your working career employers will expect you to shoulder much of the responsibility for building your retirement savings. Here's how to get started:

◆ Even though that retirement seems a long, long way off, contribute early to an individual retirement account (IRA), company 401(k) retirement plan, Keogh plan, or SEP IRA for the self-employed. Make the maximum contribution.

✦ Realize that time really pays off in the long run. A $100 monthly deposit compounding at 9 percent interest amounts to $7,599 after five years, $67,290 after twenty years, and $471,643 after forty years.

✦ With increasing job-hopping in the work world, your retirement investment will become portable. Whenever leaving a position, be sure to move your money within the necessary time limits into a rollover IRA. Don't simply take a lump sum and spend it like a windfall profit. That would be squandering your future.

One of the new wrinkles that can help a young investor get started is the direct stock purchase plan, now offered by hundreds of companies. These plans permit do-it-yourselfers to buy stock directly from companies, bypassing a broker in the process. You're able to enter into a plan in which money can be automatically deducted from your savings account, with the added ability to buy more shares in lump sums at certain intervals. Some of the most recent growth in these plans involves foreign firms that offer American Depositary Receipts on U.S. exchanges. Long-term investors can enter a plan with the intent to buy more shares without having to buy the initial share through a broker, as a traditional dividend reinvestment plan requires. Companies are basically trying to retain registered shareholders and diversify their shareholder base. Many of these plans permit you to buy stocks weekly or even daily, with the ability to sell your shares over the telephone in a transaction that's over within 24 hours.

The direct stock purchase plan is not a free lunch, however. They tend to cost more than traditional dividend reinvestment plans. About two-thirds of the companies offering them require an initial enrollment fee, as well as a fee per transaction. A small number also exact an administration fee. Worse yet, some also charge a fee on reinvestment of dividends.

Yet even with the fees, the direct stock purchase plan remains well-designed for an individual who wants to buy stock in a specific company over a period of time in small amounts. Putting even $25 or $50 a month into a plan breeds discipline and can mean a significant financial gain. The DRIP (Dividend Reinvestment Plan) Investor (800-233-5922), 7412 Calumet Ave., Hammond, Ind. 46324 provides a free listing of all companies with direct purchase plans, their phone numbers and investment minimums. Beyond your "wits and clean reputation," money socked aside for the future is a must for a young investor. Then you, too, can be content with your prospects.

34
PLAN ON MAKING MORE MONEY IN THE FUTURE

"There are written laws—they perish; but there are also unwritten laws—they are eternal. Take the unwritten law of wages: it says they've got to advance, little by little, straight through the centuries. And notice how it works. We know what wages are now, here and there and yonder; we strike an average, and say that's the wages of today. We know what the wages were a hundred years ago, and what they were two hundred years ago; that's as far back as we can get, but it suffices to give us the law of progress, the measure and rate of the periodical augmentation; and so, without a document to help us, we can come pretty close to determining what the wages were three and four and five hundred years ago. Good, so far. Do we stop there? No. We stop looking backward; we face around and apply the law to the future. My friends,

I can tell you what people's wages are going to be at any date in the future you want to know, for hundreds and hundreds of years.

(A Connecticut Yankee in King Arthur's Court)

Time, in this case its long-term effect on wages, is a major preoccupation in Mark Twain's science fiction time-travel novel. A nineteenth-century Hartford working man, Hank Morgan, is miraculously transported to sixth-century Britain and the legendary Court of King Arthur, where he puts his own technology, economics, and politics into place over a ten-year period. In this quote, he is about to explain to the town blacksmith how wages will grow over the coming 700 years, the accuracy of his predictions aided considerably by the fact he was born and lived in that future time. A stock board, insurance, factories, batteries, and even advertising become a part of the new medieval society he creates. Alas, his new civilization was not to endure. Before the wizard Merlin puts him to sleep for thirteen centuries, Hank's visit ends with 25,000 knights dying on a battlefield of wired electric fences, Gatling guns, and land mines. The book, besides its colorful mix of medieval ideals with modern technology, is a scathing indictment of institutions believed to support monarchy and slavery, including the church.

Yes, wages do move up. Even a decade ago, however, it would have been difficult to predict today's remarkable salaries that have more to do with demand and skills than with inflation. The growth of the Internet economy and a tight job market combined to kick off the millennium as an era in which the employee is in the driver's seat. In many new fields, so many people are being hired that length of experience and salary history isn't as crucial as it once was. People are more flexible in accepting new positions, especially when the carrot of incentive stock options is dangled. Remember, however, that salary gains and strong employment move in cycles in every industry. Most salary trends are ultimately determined by inflation, turnover within the industry, and competition sparked by other aggressive companies.

Always conscious of salary, Twain reportedly earned a dollar a word for his writing. A jokester once enclosed a dollar bill with a note to him that said, "Please send me a word." The reply from Twain contained one word: "Thanks."

Here are ways to improve your chances in the salary game:

+ Know what you're worth in the marketplace. Read classified ads, talk to others in your field, and examine the occupational compensation surveys of the Bureau of Labor Statistics for your region and field.

+ Compare your responsibilities to those of similar jobs at other companies. Be absolutely sure of what those positions entail, so that you'll be comparing apples to apples.

+ Keep up to date on the latest trends and technology, whatever your job may be. This not only will help you advance in your existing firm, but will make you attractive to other potential employers. Whatever your age, show an interest in being a part of fast-paced change, not someone who considers himself a "dinosaur" (remember, they became extinct).

◆ Determine whether your current management is above-board in its discussions of its overall salary levels versus the competition. That kind of reality check will also help you decide whether its promises about the future are valid.

◆ Whenever you consider a new job, be sure to look into how secure the firm is in its industry and the overall economy. Also find out about the cost of living you'll encounter in the area if you join the firm. A job may not be forever these days, but it should at least be for a while. If a company folds or announces massive layoffs as soon as times turn tough, you may not have a quick transition to a comparable position.

◆ Learn exactly how benefits, 401(k) plans, and pension plans work, as well as how often salaries are examined by management. What criteria is used to determine whether you'll be paid more?

You don't have to forecast what your progeny will likely be earning centuries from now, but you should make a career plan that takes into account financial remuneration. Know whether you're being paid what you should be paid, figure how much you'll need to reach your goals, and choose a path that will get you there. Even Camelot didn't last forever, but careful planning can provide you with the security of knowing that you have an important role in your fate. Also be realistic, for as Twain pointed out: "Even Noah got no salary for the first six months—partly on account of the weather and partly because he was learning navigation."

35
EVERY PERIOD IN HISTORY HAD FOOL'S GOLD

"One plan of acquiring sudden wealth was to 'salt' a wild cat claim and sell out while the excitement was up. The process was simple. The schemer located a worthless ledge, sunk a shaft on it, bought a wagon load of rich 'Comstock' ore, dumped a portion of it into the shaft and piled the rest by its side, above ground. Then he showed the property to a simpleton and sold it to him for a high figure."

(Roughing It)

The "greenhorn" unschooled in investment basics has always been a prime target for crooks, with the glitter of precious metals an especially effective enticement. It didn't just start with the California Gold Rush, where Mark Twain learned the ropes. As early as 2500 B.C., gold, silver, and copper were used to pay for goods and services in Egypt and Asia Minor. Over the centuries, not only were kingdoms won and lost in battles for ownership rights to hoards of precious metals, but schemes and trickery abounded.

Today, the inducements come in the form of radio, television, and Internet advertisements proclaiming that the price of one precious metal or another "is at historic lows and about to explode!" You are offered a "dramatic opportunity to participate in unparalleled profits" through purchase of the actual metal or futures contracts that bet on the future direction of its price. These ads do not change, whether the metal has been at a low for years or has been jumping about wildly lately. They count on the fact that you don't really know anything about precious metals and are therefore a "simpleton," as Twain put it. In other cases, you may receive a cold telephone call asking you to invest immediately. Don't believe this silliness or be concerned that you have only one chance to act. Precious metals have been around forever and will be for as long as man can see into the future. Furthermore, besides potential deals that may not deliver what's promised, you must realize that even conventionally sold precious metals haven't been all that great of an investment for a long time.

The true believer in precious metals wants only the actual metal itself, in the belief that in a world catastrophe only tangible assets will have any value. Such believers may keep the metal under the bed or in the crawl space while waiting for such economic disruptions. While these metals may help you one day buy bread if all goes awry with the world, they are extremely volatile in price. For example, the price of an ounce of gold was more than $600 at the beginning of 1980, less than $400 at the beginning of 1990, and less than $300 at the beginning of 2000—hardly a rewarding investment. And while gold once served as a hedge against economic disruptions, political upheaval, and runaway inflation, it has in recent years had a mind of its own that doesn't necessarily run with or counter to other trends. Due to its risk factor, experts maintain that no more than 5 to 10 percent of an individual's investment portfolio ever be placed in precious metals. After all, they don't earn interest or pay dividends while you're waiting for their price to go up.

If you still want to give precious metals a try, they're readily available in the following forms:

+ Actual metal bars available through many big banks, brokerage firms, and major dealers. Remember that you have to store them somewhere!

+ Bullion certificates sold at a 3 percent premium over the metal itself.

+ Bullion coins such as the American Gold Eagle and those minted by numerous other countries. These sell at various premiums.

+ Mining company stocks and mutual funds specializing in mining stocks. These tend to rise in price more quickly than gold itself and drop with similar speed. You must also factor in the political and industry trends associated with individual mining firms. In the case of a mutual fund, you also have to consider how adept the manager is at picking the right stocks.

+ There are options on metals and mining stocks, which are the contractual right to buy or sell that enable you to control a large amount of stock with a small amount of capital for a fixed time period. In addition, futures contracts let you bet on the future direction of metals prices. Keep in mind that you can lose your entire investment if you bet wrong.

Gold, of course, is the most familiar precious metal, while silver is an industrial metal controlled by supply and demand, and platinum is an important ingredient in production of automobile catalytic converters. With all three, avoid high-pressure sales tactics and realize that you're dealing with the most volatile of investments. And, by the way, if somebody tries to sell you a gold mine, head for the hills.

36

JOIN THE CLUB AND
PROFIT FROM IT

> "It were not best that we should all think alike; it is a
> difference of opinion that makes horse-races."
>
> *(Pudd'nhead Wilson)*

The reasons behind the apparent differences and similarities in people always fascinated Mark Twain. He was especially attracted to the concept of young people from different walks of life changing places. In *The Prince and the Pauper*, Britain's young Prince Edward accidentally changes places with commoner Tom Canty. No one notices the switch. Edward learns much about life from his time spent with the poor, then becomes a more compassionate king upon assuming the throne. In *Pudd'nhead Wilson*, slave and free babies are switched in infancy and grow up to lead very different lives. The result demonstrates the impact of training on character and the debilitating power of prejudice on people's lives. Clearly, in Twain's mind, differing backgrounds and mindsets provide intrigue in our lives.

For the investor, differing opinions are key to making wise decisions. You should never be left simply to your own devices.

In volatile times, investment clubs made up of diverse members can help solidify your ideas. The National Association of Investors Corp. has around 40,000 clubs with more than 700,000 members, all dedicated to learning about stocks and investing intelligently with that knowledge. Each club researches, discusses, or argues, tosses money into the kitty, and buys stock based on a consensus vote. Some club members want to take risks, while others want to play it safe. Some want to buy lots of stocks, and others prefer taking a slow route.

The national organization urges members to invest a sum regularly over a long period of time; reinvest earnings and dividends; learn how to select companies that have a reasonable prospect of being worth substantially more in five years; and diversify their investments. It chafes at paying too much for stocks, which rules out some sexy high-fliers. While the natural tendency of a club is to stick with familiar big-name stocks, NAIC top brass contends it's important to branch out, putting a third of money in mid-sized firms and a third in small caps, too.

The three basic considerations in forming an investment club are:

+ The members enjoy one another's company, since this is designed to be a long-term program.

+ They agree on the basic kind of investment philosophy they wish to follow, in order to avoid fundamental disagreement later.

+ All are prepared to investigate and analyze securities and make periodic reports. This isn't just a "night out." Everyone should be prepared to back up their case for buying, holding, or selling a particular equity before it's put to a vote before the entire club.

While the goal is really education and camaraderie, sometimes the profits can add up. For example, the Mutual Investment Club of Detroit has patiently invested through bull and bear markets. Founded with $800 from its members a half-century ago, it now has an investment pot of more than $6 million. The National Association of Investors Corp., P.O. Box 220, Royal Oak, Mich. 48068, requires $40 for club membership, plus $14 per member. Toll-free number is 877-ASK-NAIC. Membership includes a magazine; low-cost dividend reinvestment plan; investor information reports; and regional chapters that hold seminars and workshops, and help new clubs get started.

If you join a club, you may be astonished to find that some perfectly intelligent, thoughtful, clever people have the gall to disagree with you about specific investments. Hold on tight: The experience could make for a real horse race.

A GOOD OPPORTUNITY

The Adventures of Tom Sawyer

37
RELATIVES AND MONEY SIMPLY DO NOT MIX

"I am so superstitious that I have always been afraid to have business dealings with certain relatives and friends of mine because they were unlucky people. All my life I have stumbled upon lucky chances of large size, and whenever they were wasted it was because of my own stupidity and carelessness."

Orion Clemens, older brother of Mark Twain, fit the definition of unlucky relative quite nicely. Everything he touched seemed to spell failure. The hardworking, honest Orion did give his younger brother Sam his first newspaper job and had him serve as his assistant when he was secretary of the Nevada territory. But Twain eventually wound up supporting the quixotic Orion, who went from job to job, religion to religion, and political affiliation to political affiliation, through much of his life. "He was the strangest compound that ever got mixed in a human mold," Twain wrote of Orion in his autobiography. "Such a person as that is given to acting upon impulse and without reflection; that was Orion's way."

The financial legacy of the pair's father, John Clemens, was unlucky as well. An attorney, he had a string of failed business deals and died of pneumonia while campaigning for the post of circuit court clerk, leaving his family almost penniless. This obviously was not a family heritage around which to build great wealth. Twain was unlikely to get too excited about his brother's latest "opportunity."

Twain came about his apprehensiveness the hard way, but other people should probably be just as careful. Countless Americans who wouldn't rely on the advice of a relative or friend about what movie to see will take at face value the tips they provide about investments. Poor selections or worthless scams often blight the portfolios of many relatives and pals because word-of-mouth about the "sure thing" moved ever-so-quickly and no one wanted to miss the boat.

Employ these guidelines in family and friend investment dealings:

- ✦ Use the same due diligence that you would for any investment, checking out the company involved, the history of the individual offering the investment, and the potential risks. Uncle Harry may have helped you learn to ride a bicycle, but that doesn't mean you should shell out money based on a tip he heard at work.

- ✦ Be careful about projects that pool the money of several family members or friends. Unless you have complete confidence that you're all on the same page regarding the opportunity, that you'll be able to communicate about it as it unfolds, and that there won't be recriminations if all does not go well, leave the project alone. Throwing major money issues into relationships can prove disastrous.

+ If a deal is a partnership, take into account the potential implications of divorce or broken friendships. Would these jeopardize the entire arrangement? If so, have an attorney draft restrictions and scenarios to keep the plan viable in the face of possible disruption.

+ Never wildly toss rumors or investment long-shots around with family and friends unless you characterize them as just that, or have done some of your own homework and can honestly say the investments are worth seriously considering. Nothing is worse than seeing someone you care about lose big money because of something you spouted off about.

Nobody's perfect. While Twain himself made errors in precious metals speculation, inventions, businesses, and missed opportunities in stocks that proved to be bonanzas for others, he had only himself to blame. In his writing and speeches, he rued wasted chances due to his "stupidity and carelessness." Much of his own common sense approach to money later in life came from his own experiences, giving us all an opportunity to learn from his lesson.

"IT WAS TOM SAWYER."

Adventures of Huckleberry Finn

38

DRESS FOR SUCCESS, NOT EXCESS

"Clothes make the man. Naked people have little or no influence in society."

While his statement was made before the commercial nudity of Playboy magazine left its impressive financial impression, Mark Twain's practice of wearing the right clothes and the right look can still have positive economic consequences. The white-suited (even in winter later in his life despite his daughter's protests), physically-fit Twain always looked like a million bucks. In his younger days, he wrote a letter describing himself as "5 ft. 8 1/2 inches tall; weight about 145 pounds, sometimes a bit under, sometimes a bit over; dark brown hair and red moustache, full face with very high ears and light gray beautiful beaming eyes and a damned good moral character." Whether he was in a period flush with cash or not, he viewed looking good to be a worthwhile investment of time and money.

Today, a walk down Wall Street or through the banking or legal corridors of this country still finds well-groomed, well-dressed professionals who obviously are willing to spend what it takes to have "the look." Dressing for success, which translates to dressing for what you want to become one day, still lives. Quality pin-striped suits, designer ties, and fashionable shoes hold court for men at many firms. So do sophisticated dresses, suit ensembles, designer scarves, and Italian shoes for women. This has, however, been blunted a bit by the phenomenon known as "dress-down Fridays," which provides a modern office worker with an opportunity to "be yourself." One New York investment firm has only one real requirement for these casual days: no beach wear or swimsuits permitted. You do have to draw the line somewhere! However, even with dress-down days, the desire to be seen favorably by management remains strong. Some staffers have spent small fortunes on expensive yet casual shirts, pants, and dresses (often costing easily as much as a conventional suit or dress) that will still give them the look of upward working-place mobility, rather than the appearance of someone heading to a college "kegger."

All of this clothing philosophy breaks down today in the case of many New Economy firms in the dot-com sector and other groups. Here the emphasis, from top management on down, is on an easy-going "campus" environment and the accompanying look that can include—to varying degrees— jeans, denim skirts, work shirts, knit shirts, sweaters, loafers, and running shoes. The belief is that considerably more bright ideas and inspired work will come from those who aren't encumbered by thoughts of protocol. This is the same philoso-phy behind "equal" cubicles rather than offices based on one's relative power within the company. Each company knows what works best for it.

With all of this in mind, remember that:

◆ No matter what your work environment may be, you'll still be judged to some degree by how you look. Having a casual day or a leisure-style office is not automatic permission to come off looking like a slob. Some people wear ripped jeans to the office that they wouldn't consider wearing anywhere else. Whatever that statement may be, it isn't helping your cause.

◆ Grooming, even if you're casually dressed, is still important. Don't use relaxed policy as an opportunity not to comb your hair or wear clean clothes. No matter what the ground rules, outlandish or unkempt looks are a negative.

◆ If your work environment requires more traditional attire, don't feel you have to go hopelessly into debt to keep up with your coworkers. Buying quality basic garments that will go with a number of looks and using accessories to embellish them can get the job done. Shop sales and outlet stores. It often seems that people who carefully shop for deals get much more enjoyment out of their wardrobe anyway.

Twain always looked put together, and also took pride in the fact that he tried to stay trim. One assumes that if he worked in a leisure office today he'd be well turned out with stylish clothes appropriate to the task. By the way, he also had advice for women: "No woman can look as well out of fashion as in it."

ONE OF MY FAILURES.

Roughing It

39

YOUR FINANCIAL PLANNER CAN BAIL YOU OUT

"Beautiful credit! The foundation of modern society."

(The Gilded Age)

Mark Twain had his very own "financial planner" to help him overcome his personal credit woes. Henry Huttleston Rogers, a powerful Standard Oil Company executive and a wealthy industrialist with a net worth of $100 million, was an admirer of Twain's writing. Rogers shrewdly had Twain's wife Livy declared primary creditor of Twain's publishing firm and fashioned a repayment plan to pay off all of Twain's debts. Rogers managed Twain's business finances when he lived overseas and also negotiated book contracts for him. The two became close personal friends, drinking, playing poker, and going yachting together. "He it was who arranged with my creditors to allow me to roam the face of the earth for four years and persecute the nations thereof with lectures, promising that at the end of four years I would pay dollar for dollar," Twain said of Rogers in a dinner speech. "That arrangement was made; otherwise I would now be living out-of-doors under an umbrella, and a borrowed one at that."

When someone once commented that it was a shame Rogers' money was "tainted" due to his industrialist background, Twain replied: "That's right. 'Taint yours, and 'taint mine."

A less-than-trustworthy money counselor could spell disaster. Consider the case of a club-hopping New York financial adviser to glamorous clients such as actors Matt Damon, Ben Affleck, and Leonardo DiCaprio and rock musicians from groups such as the B-52s, Smashing Pumpkins, and Phish. Hit with criminal and civil charges that $20 million in client money was illegally transferred and $6 million was stolen, that $100 million advisory business had its assets frozen by a federal judge. Even though it once had even been in a joint venture with a prominent New York bank's private-equity business, it eventually eroded into an asset-kiting scheme in which complaining clients were paid off with money from other clients. Having a lot of money does not assure investment success if you don't do your homework in advance and keep track of your money on an ongoing basis.

Not everyone can count on someone like Twain's friend Rogers, but everyone should have a comprehensive financial plan for their family in place that includes money goals, budget, tax strategy, insurance, asset allocation, retirement plan, and a consideration of an estate plan. A planner can help you put together a detailed plan with dates and the necessary savings plan to meet your goals. Many times, the planner will immediately see the chinks in your financial armor and can provide help immediately. You may pay anywhere from $500 to $10,000 for a plan. Your net worth, the specific planner, the amount of time that must be spent on putting the plan together, and the planner's commission schedule will dictate how much you pay. Don't be bowled over by a fancy binder, graphics, and type faces. Anyone with software can make a plan look good. It's what it says that matters. In addition, realize that an effective planner can come from a variety of different professional backgrounds.

Here's what you should consider in selecting a financial planner:

+ Some financial planners charge fees only, while others sell products. Still others do both. Fee-only planners who charge by the hour are often the most reasonably-priced choice. If the planner will actively manage your money, there may be an annual asset-based fee of 0.5 percent to 1.5 percent of your assets. If the planner directs you to mutual funds, you may be paying additional fees for the funds themselves. When the planner sells products from which he derives commissions, that must be explained up front so you can determine whether the advice received is colored by that fact.

+ Professional designations are a plus. The certified financial planner (CFP) certification requires experience and a rigorous two-day examination. Check with the CFP Board of standards by calling toll-free 888-CFP-MARK to find out if the planner has credentials and whether any disciplinary action has been taken. The Chartered Financial Consultant (ChFC) designation, typically given to insurance agents, also requires experience and testing. Contact the American Society of CLU & ChFC toll-free at 888-ChFC-CLU.

◆ Major planner organizations include the National Association of Personal Financial Advisors at 800-366-2732, which has fee-only CFPs as its members; the Institute of Certified Financial Planners at 800-282-7526, which includes both fee-only and commission CFPs; and the International Association for Financial Planning at 888-806-PLAN, which includes not only CFPs, but accountants, stockbrokers, lawyers, and others.

Find out all the basics at a first get-acquainted no-cost meeting with the planner. Professional organizations will help connect you with one in your area and you should also ask friends about service they've received from local planners. Ask tough questions about the planner's credentials, experience, education, and specialties within the profession. Determine the investment style and whether specific investments will actually be recommended. Ask for professional references. It's worth the extra effort. When you start using the services of a planner, be sure to keep yourself up-to-date on investment trends so that you'll be able to intelligently make decisions with the planner's assistance. Twain's life was turned around by Rogers' help, and many people today enjoy similar boosts from their planners. With your financial house in order, credit woes and other concerns can be put in the rear-view mirror.

40
INQUIRING MINDS
WANT TO KNOW

"We like to read about rich people in the papers; the papers know it, and they do their best to keep this appetite liberally fed. . . . 'Rich Woman Fell Down Cellar—Not Hurt.' The falling down the cellar is of no interest to us when the woman is not rich, but no rich woman can fall down cellar and we not yearn to know all about it and wish it was us."

And this was before the tabloid gossip sheets and TV grabbed hold of the public consciousness. Mark Twain did enjoy his own worldwide celebrity, joking in a speech that "If it can be proved that my fame reaches to Neptune and Saturn that will satisfy me." Of course, his fame didn't just reinforce his place in history or literature, but helped him receive higher fees for his lectures as well. Once, a birthday card was mailed abroad addressed to "Mark Twain, God Knows Where." The sender several weeks later received a telegram from Italy with the words "He did."

All of this was child's play compared to today's intense scrutiny of the rich and famous. When super-wealthy television comedian Jerry Seinfeld paid a reported $40 million to buy super-wealthy pop singer/songwriter Billy Joel's mansion in 2000, the story was relayed around the planet. Will Ivanka, daughter of super-wealthy entrepreneur Donald Trump, decide to become a model? Does the home of richest-of-them-all Microsoft chairman Bill Gates really have the most square feet of any active residence? What helps more with super-wealthy talk-show hostess Oprah Winfrey's weight control, her exercise regimen or her diet? Inquiring minds want to know!

It was Twain's belief not only that we had little worthwhile to learn from the rich, but that much of what we heard about them was truly boring. "Let me tell you about the very rich," novelist F. Scott Fitzgerald noted. "They are different from you and me." However, Twain wouldn't necessarily buy into society's fascination with how different they might conceivably be. There is also within the investment world a desire to believe that some of the successful drink from a magic elixir that we may be able to mix on our own, much like a high-powered sports drink. In *Trump: The Art of the Deal*, Donald Trump wrote of his philosophy for real estate success. When his fortunes waned, there was a brief respite from his advice. His coffers refilled, he launched *Trump: The Art of the Comeback* to explain how he revived his empire. When he was pondering a presidential run, *The America We Deserve* was the result. While avid readers are now well aware of Trump's philosophies, they should simply read them with interest, rather than feel locked into adhering religiously to his precepts for one's own life and business dealings. Pick up advice here and there, realizing that even the experts have their ups and downs.

Billionaire investor Warren Buffett has similarly been lionized, with books and articles noting the remarkable success of his Omaha-based Berkshire Hathaway Inc. When his 1999 performance was sub-par, he owned up to it. "Even Inspector Clouseau could find last year's guilty party—your chairman," Buffett wrote in his annual report. But he noted that investor expectations were destined to become more realistic, especially in sectors where speculation was concentrated. Does this mean that all the talk about Buffett's genius were poppycock? Not at all. It simply once again points out that all humans are indeed human.

When viewing the lifestyles and investment observations of the super-wealthy or super-successful through the media, remember that:

✦ Everyone's experience will have something you can learn from. Try to find what might apply to your circumstances, rather than paste point-by-point advice onto your lifestyle.

✦ Don't feel in awe of those who have succeeded, or envy them, or be angry with them, or wish them ill. Don't imagine them as either sublime or miserable. There are plenty of examples of both. Live your own life and make it the best you can.

✦ Consider how you'd put together your own philosophy for success. Do you have one? If so, fine-tune its steps to see whether they're really capable of taking you anywhere.

One word of advice: If you do in fact become rich and famous, try to be more low-key than actor Sean Penn was during his ill-fated marriage to Madonna. Punching photographers only gets you into legal trouble. And the headlines are murder!

41
SOME ARE BONDED TO SUCCESS

"The world seems to think that the love of money is 'American'; and that the made desire to get suddenly rich is 'American.' I believe that both of these things are merely and broadly human, not American monopolies at all. The love of money is natural to all nations, for money is a good and strong friend. I think that this love has existed everywhere, ever since the Bible called it the root of all evil.

"I think that the reason why we Americans seem to be so addicted to trying to get rich suddenly is merely because the opportunity to make promising efforts in that direction has offered itself to us with a frequency out of all proportion to the European experience."

Many of the American fortunes made both in Mark Twain's time and in modern times were built on the stability of the most basic of investments. He fully realized there was no magic wand to make it all happen. "This is a world where you get nothing for nothing," he wrote in his autobiography, "where you pay value for everything you get and 50 per cent over; and when it is gratitude you owe, you have to pay a thousand." Bonds, which are basically long-term IOUs that pay a fixed interest rate, are financial building blocks designed to give you back what you put in, and then some. When your bond comes due, your capital is repaid in full, so a $5,000 bond is worth $5,000 upon maturity so long as the issuer doesn't default on the payment. That's simple enough. You're generally rewarded with higher rates the longer the number of years you're willing to commit. You also have the flexibility of choosing between corporate and government bonds. Bonds, however, have paled in comparison to the booming stock market and are often considered best for individuals nearing retirement or already in it, as well as for large institutions that have enormous diversified portfolios.

Modern bonds have faced a variety of factors, such as dramatic world events and sudden rate fluctuations, that have made their underlying values less predictable. That means your smartest course of action is probably to "ladder" individual bonds over a range of maturities, some as short as two years, others five to 10 years, and, if you can bear greater volatility, some up to 30 years. Shorter-term bonds are less affected by interest rate moves. While many investors prefer the highest-quality issues, more aggressive investors favor lower-quality or lowest-quality "junk" issues for the highest fixed rates of all. Also keep in mind that bonds can be "called," meaning they're recalled when the issuer wants to issue new bonds at a lower interest rate.

When considering bond investing, keep in mind that:

✦ Bonds have credit risk, in that the company issuing the bond could default and you could lose your principal investment. There is also interest rate risk, which affects you primarily if you try to sell the bond before its maturity because the value of your bond could be higher or lower, depending on where prevailing rates are at that moment.

✦ Corporate bonds and some municipal bonds are rated by agencies such as Standard & Poor's and Moody's. The highest rating is AAA or Aaa, depending on the rating system. Anything below B is considered a higher-risk "junk" bond.

✦ There are zero-coupon bonds issued by firms, government agencies, or municipalities. They don't pay interest periodically, but rather are purchased at a discount and pay a higher rate when they reach maturity. These are often used to plan for college or retirement.

✦ Municipal bonds offer tax-free advantages, especially if you're in a higher tax bracket. Various government entities issue them and they are free from federal—and in some cases state—taxes. So, if a rate seems lower than a taxable rate, you must factor in your individual tax bracket to find out what you'll ultimately receive after-tax.

✦ There are also mutual funds that invest in a pool of bonds. Such funds vary in the maturity of the bonds they hold. Some are two- to three-year parking lots, while long-term bond funds carry the same volatility of the bonds themselves. The fees that you pay on these funds is even more crucial than with stock funds because your yield is likely less to begin with. For this reason, individual bonds have tended to outperform bond funds in recent years.

Bonds, and especially bond mutual funds, aren't as influential as they once were. Some portfolio strategists don't include them at all in their model portfolios, contending that interest rate fluctuations make them as potentially volatile as stocks. But while they may no longer make you rich, they can still be a viable tool for capital preservation if properly incorporated into an overall portfolio. Municipal bonds in particular can be great tax-savers. But always run the numbers to determine if bonds will work for you.

42

GOVERNMENT WOULD
GIVE GOD A BAD NAME

> "There was never a nation in the world that put its
> whole trust in God. . . . I think it would better read,
> 'Within certain judicious limitations we trust in God,'
> and if there isn't enough room on the coin for this,
> why, enlarge the coin."

Any distrust of government and politicians was distrust well-spent, according to Mark Twain. It's little surprise that he found that the government's use of God's name in national coinage had a veneer of hypocrisy. Not only did he question politicians' moral fiber, but he wrote that "Politician and idiot are synonymous terms" and "Public office is private graft." Twain was especially outraged at the corruption he saw in New York's Tammany Hall while he lived there and wrote about it often. In his book *The Gilded Age*, which preached about the futility of chasing after wealth, an especially pious Missouri politician, Senator Abner Dilworthy, is found to be corrupt after buying votes to try to ensure his reelection. Twain was similarly leery of organized religion. While not an atheist, he generally preferred the basic concepts of God and nature's laws to the various regimented ways of worshipping. "What God lacks is convictions—stability of character," he wrote. "He ought to be a Presbyterian or a Catholic or something,—not try to be everything."

At the modern prayer breakfast, God is often praised by politicians and business people alike for his largesse in producing record corporate profits, strong stock markets, and solid economic growth, in much the same way he is praised for helping football teams win big games. Mercifully, God usually escapes any accusations of blame for the bankruptcy rate, market corrections, or recessions. But then politicians and business people don't blame themselves for those events either, rather insisting that these things "just happen" in the natural course of things. Twain did not chide God, but he did chastise those who would elevate themselves by evoking God's name, and preferred to have God speak for himself through religious literature. Just as Twain poked fun at himself, he used humor to put everyone else in their place as well. He once referred to his close friend Joseph Twichell as "one of the best of men, although a clergyman."

43

A NEW DEAL FOR SHAREHOLDERS WAS OVERDUE

President Franklin Delano Roosevelt reportedly took the name "New Deal" for his economic program to pull the nation out of the Depression from this portion of *Connecticut Yankee:* "I was to become a stockholder in a corporation where nine hundred and ninety-four of the members furnished all the money and did all the work, and the other six elected themselves a permanent board of directors and took all the dividends. It seemed to me that what the nine hundred and ninety-four dupes needed was a new deal."

Just as FDR's New Deal helped jumpstart a Depression economy in the 1930s, in modern times the concept of the company board of directors has been jumpstarted as well. In Mark Twain's time, it was sometimes "anything goes" and shareholders could be at the mercy of a greedy, all-powerful board. This group of individuals elected by the shareholders traditionally directs and oversees

the affairs of the corporation and monitors the action of corporate officers. It also sets dividend policy for a company,
which can be an indicator of growth in earnings and revenue.
As recently as a couple of decades ago, a directorship was still a
cushy job that paid extremely well for only a few days spent on
doing very little company business each year. There was little
accountability then, but times change.

The modern investor-rights movement has put boards of
directors on the hot seat, accountable for how their actions
affect stock prices, pension funds, and the health of the company. Legal action has been taken in numerous cases against
directors in recent years for not monitoring a company's
actions or for permitting policies detrimental to shareholders.
The era of the "rubber stamp" board is disappearing because
each individual board member has responsibility. In addition,
insider trading by directors and officers of companies is monitored closely. Insider trading is a stock transaction by an officer
or director of a company whose stock is traded, or by any individual or entity holding 10 percent or more of any class of the
company's shares. Specific types of activity include sale, buy,
planned sale, and exercise of options. The Securities and
Exchange Commission watches these transactions closely to
monitor for impropriety, while investors want to see what kind
of a statement they make about the firm's prospects.

Some corporate boards maintain stellar reputations. The
best, as rated by *Fortune* magazine, are those of General
Electric, which regularly updates its board with new outside
directors; Home Depot, which requires each director to make
formal visits to at least 20 of its stores annually; Intel, whose
directors aren't allowed to receive additional consulting fees

from the company; and Texas Instruments, whose directors have overseen a successful reinvention of the company. Among the worst boards, according to the magazine, are those of Advanced Micro Devices, which gave an overly generous 33-page employment contract to its CEO that includes a performance bonus after he's dead; Archer Daniels Midland, which merely put a senior vice president on leave while he served a two-year prison sentence for price-fixing; Maxxam, which moved its annual meeting to a remote location 20 miles from the nearest hotel to avoid potential dissent from environmentalists; and Ogden, whose board does not have one CEO of a for-profit company.

As an aware shareholder, you must make certain that you don't simply follow any board's directives blindly.

◆ Read carefully each proposal in the proxy statements you receive from the company so you can decide how to vote your shares. This is key to understanding what the company is up to and how it might affect your holdings.

◆ Try to attend annual meetings when you can, especially in the case of firms that rotate such meetings among regions from year to year. This provides a free education on the machinations of corporate executives and boards. Even if it is highly orchestrated, you will find out "who's who" and undoubtedly there will be questions asked by participating shareholders.

◆ You may wish to have your shares registered in your own name so you can best participate in company decision-making by being sure to receive all company materials. It is all right to have your shares registered in "street name" through your broker, just so long as you're receiving company literature and data in a timely fashion so you do have the opportunity to vote your shares by mail.

Shareholders have their "new deal." But taking full advantage of it requires your close attention and participation so you can avoid being one of those "dupes" Twain wrote about. Twain himself was to become a corporate board member later in life. One assumes those meetings were seldom boring!

44

YOU STILL CAN'T TELL
A BOOK BY ITS COVER

"For business reasons, I must preserve the outward
signs of sanity."

While Mark Twain was kidding about needing to put up a front, he did work hard to keep everything together as he overcame adversity. He was, after all, a humorist, lecturer, and writer, and while the public could accept sarcasm, no one wanted gloom and doom from someone expected to be engaging. Great personal tragedy late in his life made it tougher to stay on an even keel. His oldest daughter Susy died of meningitis in 1895, his wife Livy passed away in 1904, and youngest daughter Jean suffered a fatal heart attack during an epileptic seizure in 1909, just months before Twain's own demise. The second of his three daughters, Clara, was the only one to survive him. She staunchly guarded her father's legacy until her death in 1962, leaving the bulk of his papers to what was to become the Mark Twain Papers at the University of California at Berkeley.

Toward the end of his life, Twain by some accounts was full of despair and pessimism, while other reports say he became kinder and more generous. He often wrote about his inner feelings and also remained a spritely commentator on world events to the end. In terms of his generosity, many signs of it were not unearthed until long after his death. For example, in 1985 a Yale scholar found documentary proof that Twain had paid for the college education of two talented black men, one who graduated from Yale Law School and became a judge and the other who graduated from seminary and became a minister. He had sought no publicity for such actions, for they were never intended to boost his public image.

Putting the best foot forward is a basic philosophy of the modern business world. Never has there been a corporate annual report or press release that didn't put the best possible spin on even the most negative of occurrences. Similarly manipulated is the image of the chief executive, more likely to be portrayed in company literature as hard-nosed and intuitive rather than annoying or frivolous, whatever the reality may be. The concept of the company as logical, forthright, and successful leaves no room for anything to appear "flaky." Public relations consultants work hard to put together the proper image for the company's leadership through coaching and placement of interviews. That image is watched closely by the investment community, employees, and the public at large, since one false move can wipe out years of carefully-crafted identity-making.

In the modern corporate image department, nothing stands out like the more than 12,000 colorful annual reports that pour into mailboxes and onto the Internet each year. They seek to put the most gloss possible on the prior year's business, often using a theme to drive home their points. Most companies have lately reduced their number of printed copies, which average more than $3 per individual copy to produce, in the belief that potential investors can easily read the information on the Web. Whatever the medium, not all companies tell their year's story accurately, in full, or cleverly, so some professional scrutiny is required. For example, Sid Cato's Newsletter on Annual Reports, P.O. Box 19850, Kalamazoo, Mich. 49019 (*www.sidcato.com*) ranks the reports, taking into account factors such as presentation, clarity, writing, information, and chief executive involvement. Meanwhile, The Annual Reports Library, 369 Broadway, San Francisco, Calif. 94133 (*www.zpub.com/sf/arl*) keeps two million annual reports on file, some from the 1940s, as it tracks trends in this important field.

Here are the sections to examine closely in each annual report:

- ✦ Chairman of the board letter, covering changing conditions, goals, and actions. Reading between the lines, is it apologizing for anything?

- ✦ Sales and marketing, which should cover what the company sells, how, where, and when. Is it clear where it makes most of its money and what the scope is of lines, divisions, and operations?

- ✦ Ten-year summary of financial figures, which should show the growth of profits and operating income.

- ✦ Management discussion and analysis, which should give a candid and accurate discussion of significant financial trends for the past *two* years.

+ Financial statements, which track sales, profits, research and development spending, inventory and debt levels over time. Read footnotes carefully!

+ Lists of directors and officers, worth examining to determine how many outside versus inside directors there are and qualifications of those directors.

+ Stock price history, showing the general price trend over time, where the stock is listed, the stock symbol, and the bonus/dividend history.

It's your job as an investor to disregard the snow job and get down to the reality of a company before you plunk down your hard-earned money. This will avoid unwanted surprises later.

45
WARNING: PRODUCT HAS POTENTIAL SIDE EFFECTS

> "'What got you into trouble?' says the baldhead to
> t'other chap. 'Well, I'd been selling an article to take
> the tartar off the teeth—and it does take it off, too,
> and generly the enamel along with it—but I staid
> about one night longer than I ought to, and was just
> in the act of sliding out when I ran across you on the
> trail this side of town, and you told me they were
> coming, and begged me to help you to get off. So I
> told you I was expecting trouble myself and would
> scatter out with you.'"
>
> *(Exchange between con men the King and the Duke
> in* Huckleberry Finn*)*

The self-proclaimed King was certainly pitching to common folks one of the more powerful forms of tartar control! These days, pitchmen don't come into town in a wagon with a case, setting up shop to present their spiel. They are more likely to appear on "infomercials," half-hour productions which look and sound like television talk shows or news reports, but are actually paid advertisements. They feature paid "experts" and moderators, in some cases celebrities. The presentation is interrupted from time to time with what seem to be "commercials" within the program. There may be a news set, a kitchen, a workout gym, or comfortable chairs to set the mood. It just "so happens" that on that particular day, the topic is a certain product. While one presenter extols its virtues, another sidekick often follows up with "wow" and "tell me more" comments. There may also be a studio audience, enthusiastically applauding the amazing results that the product produces.

Here's what you must keep in mind about infomercials:

◆ Check for the sponsor identification at the beginning or end of the infomercial, which is required by the Federal Communications Commission. Look for commercials within the infomercial that are the same as the "program" content.

◆ Be especially careful about health claims or "get rich quick" claims, both of which are mainstays of the infomercial, says the Federal Trade Commission. Consumers are especially vulnerable to such claims and advertisers play this card to the hilt.

◆ Realize that experts and celebrities endorsing products are usually paid by the advertiser, even though it seems that they're there simply because they've been bowled over by the product.

◆ If you purchase an infomercial product, you have certain protections under the Mail and Telephone Order Merchandise Rule, and the Fair Credit Billing Act if you pay by credit card. By law, a company should ship the order within the time stated in the ads. If no time is promised, the company should ship within 30 days after receiving payment.

Another concern these days is the "free" and "low-cost" personal computer offer in which the PC may not have all the components or the capacity you need, may require long-distance calls to an Internet service, and may expect you to accept additional advertising on your screen. Some of the low-cost deals require that you pay off your entire balance the first month. Know exactly how you'll be paying, the terms, and what you're getting. Rebate offers are yet another problem consumers encounter. It's best to make a copy of all paperwork you've mailed in when applying for the rebate, as well as the documentation you received when buying the item. Another trouble spot is advertising and marketing on the Internet, which is drawing scrutiny regarding potential unfair or deceptive practices. Advertiser claims must offer full details and be substantiated, with any disclaimers and disclosures "clear and conspicuous." The FTC monitors the Internet to see whether commercial web sites are posting privacy policies and honoring consumers' privacy preferences. If you have problems with various products you've purchased from television or the Internet, the FTC, your state Attorney General, and the local Business Bureau can help. You can file complaints with the FTC by contacting the Consumer Response Center toll-free at 1-877-FTC-HELP, or by mail at 600 Pennsylvania Ave. NW, Washington, D.C. 20580, or by Internet using the online complaint form.

Human nature hasn't changed since Twain's time, but there is now a more humane attitude toward the crooks than the following punishment bestowed on *Huckleberry Finn's* King and Duke:

> "Here comes a raging rush of people, with torches, and an awful whooping and yelling, and banging tin pans and blowing horns; and we jumped to one side to let them go by; and as they went by, I see they had the king and the duke astraddle of a rail—that is, I knowed it was the king and the duke, though they was all over tar and feathers, and didn't look like nothing in the world that was human—just looked like a couple of monstrous big soldier-plumes. Well, it made me sick to see it; and I was sorry for them poor pitiful rascals, it seemed like I couldn't ever feel any hardness against them any more in the world. It was a dreadful thing to see. Human beings can be awful cruel to one another."

46
INVEST WITH AN ATTITUDE: YOUR OWN

"Whenever you find that you are on the side of the majority, it is time to reform—(or pause and reflect)."

Never running with the herd, Mark Twain would pick and choose what he liked best from society and the investment world at large. He developed his attitude toward money based in large part on the hard times he had experienced, but always retained a flair for technology and the future. "The trouble with these beautiful, novel things is that they interfere so with one's arrangements," he told a reporter for the *New York Times* after a presentation of a unique electrical music maker called the telharmonium. "Every time I see or hear a new wonder like this I have to postpone my death right off."

His investment dichotomy between common sense and the futuristic aspirations fits well with twenty-first century trends. For years, average investors patiently assembled common sense portfolios built around familiar company names in diverse industries. Stock in a small retailer, for example, was considered a high-growth investment. Technology was a risky taboo, avoided by many conservative investors and portfolio managers. Times have changed dramatically and not just because tech stocks are booming at the start of a new century. There is a fundamental adjustment underway in portfolio strategy, with people of all ages choosing technology stocks for at least a portion of their holdings. You just can't get that kind of growth anywhere else. Yet it is volatile growth. Many investors have learned the hard way that these stocks do not perform in an entirely predictable manner.

The best way to get started in technology, key experts agree, is to build a foundation of quality technology companies by buying them on any price dips. From these core holdings— that emphasize popular names such as networking firm Cisco Systems Inc. (ticker symbol CSCO), cell phone maker Nokia Corp. (NOK), and semiconductor manufacturer Intel Corp. (INTC)—you can move on to developing companies that carry much greater risk and potential reward.

While you must make your own stock calls, here are some expert game plans for the next five years and beyond that reflect assorted views of our changing times:

Charles Pradilla, chief investment strategist with SG Cowen Securities:

> "I am 60 years old and don't own one Old Economy (tra-
> ditional industry) stock, preferring technology instead. If
> old economy stocks are a declining franchise with declin-
> ing penetration and are not changing the world, why
> would I want that long-term? Everything's changing too
> quickly to have a cut-and-dried model portfolio. To play

this change in a conservative way, begin by investing in companies that will play an important role the next five years, namely Cisco Systems, Microsoft (MSFT), Intel, America Online (AOL), and Hewlett-Packard (HWP). I would eat all the stock certificates of Procter & Gamble, Philip Morris, Goodyear, and Sears Roebuck if it turns out that their performance isn't beaten by those five tech stocks. Anyone with a conventional or Roth individual retirement account and a 15 to 25 year time horizon has to be in these stocks."

Hugh Johnson, chief investment officer, First Albany Corp.:

"If the market weight of the Standard & Poor's 500 is 32 percent technology, then you want to overweight technology (invest a larger percentage) in your own portfolio. Whether it becomes 35 percent or 55 percent of your portfolio depends on the amount of risk you want to assume, because you'll be reducing diversification and increasing volatility. My core technology holdings are Sun Microsystems (SUNW), International Business Machines (IBM), Oracle (ORCL), Motorola (MOT), Texas Instruments (TXN), Cisco Systems, and Microsoft. For the non-tech portion of my portfolio, I own stocks from each of the major sectors. These include basic materials firm Aluminum Co. of America (AA); consumer cyclicals Home Depot (HD) and Harley-Davidson (HDI); consumer non-cyclical PepsiCo (PEP); energy firms BP Amoco (BPA) and Exxon Mobil (XOM); financial firm Citigroup (C); drug companies Bristol-Myers Squibb (BMY) and Johnson & Johnson (JNJ); and industrials General Electric (GE), Tyco International (TYC), and United Technologies (UTX). I own no utilities. In telecommunications, I like Germany's Deutsche Telekom (DT), and Nokia."

Robert Stovall, senior market strategist with Prudential Securities:

"We have a 'fire and ice' technique, with a foot in both the tech and the non-tech camps, but the strongest-performing segments are going to be in technology. No more than 35 percent of one's portfolio should be in tech, with 15 percent even better for some folks. While Applied Materials (AMAT), Biogen (BGEN), Vitesse Semiconductor (VTSS), Motorola, and Nokia are on our recommended list, they should be balanced out with standard big companies such as Ford Motor (F), Coca-Cola (KO), and Ralston-Purina (RAL). It's tough to listen to cocktail party conversations where some guy who doesn't know a convertible bond from a convertible Saab tells you how much money he has made just buying a package of biotech stocks. That's tough to take, but prudence is the right way to play all this."

Marshall Acuff, investment strategist with Salomon Smith Barney:

"There's always going to be someone who can hit more home runs or do something better, but you must know your own risk tolerance. Because the high valuation of the stock market has helped make the cost of capital relatively inexpensive, we have many more new companies than we'd have had if the market were depressed. Even if Coca-Cola and Procter & Gamble repair themselves, they'll grow more slowly than IBM or Dell Computer (DELL). While it's important to diversify your portfolio, don't go completely overboard and pay far too much for highly valued tech companies. Playing the business-to-business theme, I like Microsoft, Cisco Systems, Oracle, Sun, and Hewlett-Packard. In communications, I prefer Nokia, Qwest Communications (QWST), and WorldCom (WCOM). I also like JDS Uniphase (JDSU), and Lucent Technologies (LU)."

Robert Walberg, chief equity strategist with the Briefing.com. online stock research firm:

> "You had the industrial revolution and now you have the birth of the technology revolution. Stock of many Old Economy leaders, such as General Electric, Home Depot, Wal-Mart Stores, and Coca-Cola, are still not cheap based on their historic norms. No matter what your age, have exposure to dynamic market sectors. If you're a conservative investor, stick with Qualcomm (QCOM), Nokia, Cisco Systems, and Intel. Then move on to developing stocks, which will be more volatile. Tech companies will withstand higher interest rates because they're not funding their growth through financing, but with stock. Rising oil prices aren't an issue for them either."

While others prefer technology mutual funds that give investors broader diversity, the trend is still toward including technology to a greater degree in one's portfolio. Toward the end of the last century, stratified portfolios with clear percentages for types of stock, bonds, and money market instruments were common. That is now changing. Don't jump at the future with such abandon that you're at its mercy, but, like Twain, be up on what's happening and don't be afraid to get involved to the degree that you remain comfortable.

STRIKING A POCKET.

Roughing It

47

MUTUAL FUND EXPENSES CAN HOODWINK YOU

"It is strange the way the ignorant and inexperienced so often and so undeservedly succeed when the informed and the experienced fail."

(Commenting on a store clerk who became rich on a stock Twain didn't buy, in The Autobiography of Mark Twain.*)*

Many Americans with little investing knowledge or experience have hit the big time over the past two decades, just as that ever-so-fortunate store clerk did in Mark Twain's day. They've racked up profits with mutual funds, a "no brainer" vehicle with easy entry that pools the money of many investors to buy stocks, bonds, or money market instruments. They're an especially good way for young people to get involved in the market with a small initial outlay of cash. The road to for novice investors has often involved very basic funds, such as the giant Fidelity Magellan Fund and the Vanguard S&P 500 Index Fund, that they've stashed in their individual retirement accounts. Often the funds chosen were heavily advertised by mutual fund companies, featured in magazine articles, or included by their employer as choices in company 401(k) retirement plans. The money was put away, put out of mind, and provided outstanding gains thanks to a powerful bull market. That's what long-term investing is all about.

However, what about periods when those funds aren't making you happy? Over the past several years, many funds haven't done well at all, in particular those with no technology holdings or those that patiently seek out stocks at low valuations. When the stock market throws some ice-cold water in your face, you begin to notice a few things, such as how much you're paying in expenses on your mutual funds. Those costs are overlooked when returns are going up, up, and away, but stand out when your fund's experiencing troubles. Examine carefully how much you're paying on your funds.

The annual expense ratio, representing a fund's cost of doing business as a percent of its assets, is the best place to start. It includes management fees and all operating costs except brokerage fees and annual account maintenance fees. Annual expense ratios below 0.5 percent are generally considered low, while those above 1.5 percent are deemed high. The average annual expense ratio of U.S. diversified stock funds is 1.43; small-cap funds, 1.59; international funds, 1.71; government bond funds, 1.09 percent; and bond funds, .94 percent. Remember that if your fund is down, say, 10 percent because the market hits a down period, and you add another 2 percent, the resulting 12 percent loss is a very big deal.

Be an active shareholder, keeping track of exactly what your funds require in expenses. If you notice other funds charging less, it's obviously something that is quite possible to accomplish.

If you go back historically, lower-cost funds tend to have higher returns than high-cost funds. Buying a low-cost fund doesn't guarantee good performance, but in certain areas, such as bond funds, it can be more important than even management skill. Furthermore, higher-cost funds sometimes take greater risks with their portfolio to try to overcome the handicap they face to begin with. Don't consider fees and expenses only, since overall performance of a fund is obviously more important, but do understand the different costs you may encounter.

These are types of transaction expenses that can be charged directly to the investor's account:

+ A front-end sales charge or "load" is attached to the initial purchase of mutual fund shares. This fee is to compensate a financial professional for his or her services. By law, this charge may not exceed 8.5 percent of the initial investment. "No-load" funds do not have these charges.

+ A contingent deferred sales charge, imposed at redemption, is another way to compensate the financial professionals for services. It typically applies for the first few years of ownership and then disappears.

+ A redemption fee is another type of back-end charge for redeeming shares. It is expressed as a dollar amount or as a percentage of the redemption price.

+ An exchange fee is the fee, if any, charged when transferring money from one fund to another within the same fund family.

Fund investors often have absolutely no idea how much of their money slips away for various reasons. Annual operating expenses reflect the costs of operating a fund and are deducted from fund assets before earnings are distributed to shareholders. Management fees are ongoing fees charged by the fund's investment advisor for managing the fund and selecting its portfolio. These fees generally average between 0.5 percent and 1 percent of the fund's assets annually. 12b-1 fees, used by some funds, are deducted from fund assets to pay for marketing and distribution expenses, such as compensating sales people. By law, 12b-1 fees used to pay marketing and distribution expenses can't exceed 0.75 percent of the fund's average net assets per year. There is also a lifetime cap on the fund's overall sales. A "no-load" fund can't have a 12b-1 fee of more than 0.25 percent.

Mutual funds have a deserved reputation as an easy way to invest that can reap substantial rewards. However, over the long haul it always pays to know what you've invested in and to watch it closely. Especially in down market periods, the cost of investing can erode the positives of this "every man" vehicle.

48
TRAVEL INTELLIGENTLY AND OFTEN

"I immediately called a hackman (carriage driver), and told him to take me to a cheap but respectable hotel. 'And the cheaper it is,' I added, 'the more respectable I shall consider it.'"

Mark Twain was an active traveler in a time when few Americans had the opportunity or finances to venture too far outside their natural surroundings. In his early days, Twain had to watch his nickels and dimes, but later his position as a writer of travel articles and books made getting around a much more comfortable proposition. Photographs of Twain relaxing in his chair on the deck of a cruise ship wearing a captain's cap contrast sharply with today's sold-out capacity airline flights, but frequent flyer and discount travel programs do extend the financial opportunity to travel to the majority of Americans. Some will see the same sights in Venice, Egypt, or other destinations that Twain enjoyed. Twain saw both the realities and the beauties of world travel. A good example of the latter is his narrator's description in *Roughing It* of approaching the Hawaiian Islands:

> "After two thousand miles of watery solitude the vision was a welcome one. As we approached, the imposing promontory of Diamond Head rose up out of the ocean, its rugged front softened by the hazy distance, and presently the details of the land began to make themselves manifest: first the line of beach; then the plumed cocoanut trees of the tropics; then cabins of the natives; then the white town of Honolulu."

Wherever you or your family may be headed, here are some important travel considerations if you want to control your budget:

✦ It pays to find a good travel agent who knows destinations and lodging, and will do a follow-up to ascertain the quality of your experience. Agents who have taken a two-year course from the Institute of Certified Travel Agents and have five years of travel industry background can call themselves Certified Travel Counsellors (CTCs). The American Society of Travel Agents (ASTA) designation means the agency has been around three years and has agreed to a code of ethics. If you have specific travel needs, seek out specialized agents who emphasize cruises, seniors, or other adventure in their business.

✦ Do your homework to find out the best means of reaching your destinations. Plan well in advance to take advantage of lower airfares, buy your ticket early, and head off the chance of being hit with a fare increase. Staying over Saturday night is a common requirement for a cheap fare, as is leaving on certain less-traveled weekdays. Be fully aware of all restrictions on any ticket you buy.

✦ If you're signing up for a tour package, be sure to check out how reputable the tour company is. More than a few travelers have been left holding the bag when the company goes belly-up or does a poor job of making the necessary arrangements.

✦ Go online to find travel deals. There are now sites that not only clue you in to the latest deals, but let you bid in order to obtain the lowest deals. Also consider discounters, known as consolidators, that offer tickets significantly below list price. When carriers can't fill seats, they sell the tickets to these consolidators at discount.

✦ Use common sense when selecting your accommodations. Don't try to work your way into a hotel at the last minute and don't make reservations at a hotel you haven't researched. An otherwise wonderful trip can turn out to be a bust if you don't enjoy where you're staying.

✦ Look into all-inclusive packages in order to save money. Also consider cruises, which include basic costs, with the exception of alcoholic beverages and the tips required by waiters and those who clean your cabin.

We have lasting memories of Twain's trips. For example, drawing upon his visit to the Great Sphinx in Egypt, Twain wrote of its sad face in *Innocents Abroad* and had his character Jim stranded on top of it as an agitated crowd tormented him in *Tom Sawyer Abroad*. However, for most of today's travelers, the memories that their photographs and videotapes conjure up must suffice. Just make sure the bills you receive upon your return don't leave an even more lasting impression on your bank account.

A SIDE SHOW

The Adventures of Tom Sawyer

49

ALWAYS COMPOUND
YOUR GOOD FORTUNE

> "The widow Douglas put Huck's money out at six per
> cent, and Judge Thatcher did the same with Tom's at
> aunt Polly's request. Each lad had an income, now,
> that was simply prodigious—a dollar for every week-
> day in the year and half of the Sundays. It was just
> what the minister got—no, it was what he was prom-
> ised—he generally couldn't collect it."
>
> *(Tom Sawyer)*

Huck and Tom would've prospered
today with the help of the widow
Douglas and Judge Thatcher. If only Americans today had
their money so well invested. The U.S. personal saving rate was
2.4 percent of income in 1999, the lowest one-year rate recorded
in more than a generation, even though the cost of future
years is getting more expensive because we live longer after we
retire. Many Americans spend 15, 25, even 30 years in retirement. We are also more active, taking advantage of many more
opportunities to spend our money through travel, dining, and
shopping. Unable to resist temptation, we're spending like

drunken sailors even though there are so many savings vehicles now available.

Dollar-cost averaging, the investing of a fixed amount in a particular stock or mutual fund account on a regular basis, is a great way to get on the road to saving and investing. You don't have to spend a lot of time fretting over what you'll invest in next. Simply resolve to methodically invest the same amount of money every month or have it taken from your paycheck or savings account. Payroll deduction plans can be a great help. Dollar-cost averaging keeps your investing on an even keel and keeps you from worrying over the ups and downs of the market. In the case of mutual funds or individual stocks, when investment value is up you can be happy that some of your holdings were bought when prices were lower. When prices go down, you have the opportunity to snap up some bargains. This gives you some gumption at a time when your confidence might otherwise be shot.

Here are some other good points about dollar-cost averaging:

✦ If you're committed to automatic investment each month, most mutual funds will waive their otherwise high initial minimum requirement. You won't have to shell out $2,500 to $3,000 and you can get started immediately.

✦ You develop discipline, even if you don't have to make a decision every month. You know that the process is continuing and that you'll reap the rewards. That's a great feeling.

✦ If you're a beginning investor, it gets you right into the action and keeps you there.

✦ While it's true that you'd do better putting in one large lump sum and watching it grow, dollar-cost averaging is a viable alternative if you don't have enough cash all at once.

✦ There is really no downside, other than making it harder to purchase some items you might be better off not buying anyway.

You don't need the widow Douglas or Judge Thatcher to keep you saving if you show a little self-discipline. Twain had his financier friend Henry Huttleston Rogers to help keep his personal finances in line, help for which he was eternally grateful: "His commercial wisdom has protected my pocket ever since in those lucid intervals wherein I have been willing to listen to his counsels and abide by his advice—a thing which I do half the time and half the time I don't."

IMPARTING INFORMATION.

Roughing It

50
HAVE A MAP FOR
THE ROAD'S END

"In order to know a community, one must observe the
style of its funerals and know what manner of men
they bury with most ceremony."

(Roughing It)

Through the death of two daughters
and his wife, Mark Twain experienced
grief and loss late in life. The final chapter of his autobiography
was entitled "The Death of Jean," in reference to his late daughter, and was a sentimental look at the loss of family and friends
he had endured. Twain made one last visit to the island of
Bermuda in failing health in early 1910. Upon his return home,
he was suffering from chest pains and passed away on April 20
of that year. Yet death was not a joyless event in his eyes. He did
not fear it and kept a sense of humor about its imminent likelihood. Regarding the proper decorum in heaven, Twain wrote
this directive shortly before his death: "Do not show off. St.
Peter dislikes it. The simpler you are dressed, the better it will
please him. He cannot abide showy costumes. Above all things,
avoid over-dressing. A pair of spurs & a fig-leaf is a plenty."

Death has not changed in modern times, but its cost has escalated. There is no shame in pricing out the various costs and seeking the best deals. No one enjoys talking about their own funeral arrangements or those of their parents, but it's an important discussion because the price of a funeral is so significant. As a supplement to your will, have a letter of instructions regarding your wishes. This includes your preferred funeral arrangements; notification of whether you're an organ donor; names and addresses of funeral home, crematory, and cemetery; details of the type of service you wish; casket and headstone choices; and your preferred death notice. The cost of a funeral is typically covered either from money set aside for that purpose, through a specific investment account, or as part of your life insurance pay-out. Don't be afraid to bargain on the costs involved in the funeral, cremation, or earth burial, since prices can vary widely.

Of course, funeral arrangements are just one consideration of an overall financial plan you should have in place prior to your death. Two out of three Americans die without a will, leaving it up to the courts to make major decisions involving their loved ones. That's not a good idea. A will is basically the legal document that transfers what you own to your beneficiaries. It pays to have a qualified attorney draw up your will to assure that there are no mistakes, loopholes, or ambiguities. They typically charge by the hour, so it's a good idea to have good records and have your thoughts in order. It's important to carefully go over all of your assets to give an accurate depiction of what you actually have. Be very, very specific about your wishes. A will may be nasty in intent, but, if it's your wishes and you were of sound mind, it will be carried out.

What you should know about a will:

+ It transfers what you own to your beneficiaries when you die.

+ It names the executor whom you wish to carry out the will's terms.

+ It names a guardian if you have minor children and possibly a trustee to handle their funds until they come of age.

+ Minor changes are made with a codicil, or written amendment.

+ What's known as a living will expresses your wishes about being kept alive if you're terminally ill or seriously injured.

If your affairs are more involved, you may wish to spend additional money to set up a trust. A trust can be worthwhile in estate planning, but is not a tax break. Many people enter into trusts unnecessarily because their wishes are already clear-cut and well-defined in their wills. A trust is basically a legal entity that earns income, pays taxes, and distributes earnings. It is administered by a trustee and can be set up to make distributions for the needs of your heirs. It can name someone to handle your money if you're incapacitated (make sure this is well-defined, such as requiring the okay of two licensed physicians) and is generally harder to challenge than a will.

Here are the basic types of trusts:

+ Living trusts are set up while you're alive; you can serve as trustee yourself, and upon your death assets are directly distributed to beneficiaries.

+ Testamentary trusts are created by your will, funded by your estate, and administered by trustees.

◆ Pour-over trusts have aspects of both and are established while you're alive in order to receive assets such as life insurance benefits that are paid at your death. They can also receive will-specified assets.

In all areas regarding your death, be sure to communicate to family members the basics so there will be no surprises later. Many remarried couples in particular want to spell out exactly who gets what to avoid controversies involving different sets of children later. Let trustees and guardians know they've been chosen and determine whether they wish to fulfill those responsibilities. Be sure to communicate where your will is located. Make sure that the listing of beneficiaries on your investment accounts and insurance policies are in line with the wishes of your will. Death comes to everyone, so handle its repercussions capably. Otherwise, there can be ongoing controversy and vindictiveness within your surviving family when you're gone. Twain certainly was at peace prior to his death. His very last statement was a memorandum about death, which he'd prepared so that the press would have something to quote: "Death, the only immortal who treats us all alike, whose pity and whose peace and whose refuge are for all—the soiled and the pure, the rich and the poor, the loved and the unloved."

Epilogue

"If you get in—If you get in—don't tip him. That is, publicly. Don't hand it to him, just leave a quarter on the bench by him, and let on you forgot it. If he bites it to see if it is good, you are not to seem to notice it."

(on tipping St. Peter upon one's arrival in Heaven, from "Etiquette for the Afterlife")

The tipping protocol in heaven was one of many otherworldly thoughts on Mark Twain's mind. His own earthly arrival and departure were dramatically etched in the stars. Born in 1835 under Halley's Comet, which reappears about every 75 years, he died during its next visit in 1910. He often noted the fact that he was born with the comet and also accurately predicted that he would one day "go out with it." Another example of his ongoing fascination with both the stars and the afterlife is his story "Captain Stormfield's Visit to Heaven." Written off and on over a 40-year period, it tells of a ship's captain who dies at sea and spends 30 years flying through space at the speed of light—which Twain dutifully notes is 186,000 miles a second—before he finally joyously lands in heaven.

No one better understood and expressed the ironies of life than Twain. Our precarious financial existence is especially unfair, he mused in a letter:

> "The whole scheme of things is turned wrong end to. Life should begin with age and its privileges and accumulations, and end with youth and its capacity to splendidly enjoy such advantages. As things are now, when in youth a dollar would bring a hundred pleasures, you can't have it. When you are old, you get it and there is nothing worth buying with it then. It's an epitome of life. The first half of it consists of the capacity to enjoy without the chance; the last half consists of the chance without the capacity."

Rich or poor, old or young, Mark Twain enjoyed all those advantages of life to their full capacity. Money was just a part of his life, but an important aspect that we can all learn from.

BIBLIOGRAPHY

This book hopefully whets the reader's appetite for even more of Mark Twain's thoughts and writing. He had something to say on darned near everything he encountered during a long and varied lifetime, and he said it well. Quotes from Twain's own works at the beginning of a chapter are identified as such. Other Twain quotes were culled from reliable reference books about the author's speeches and letters. Specifically, *The Wit and Wisdom of Mark Twain*, edited by Alex Ayres; *The Quotable Mark Twain: His Essential Aphorisms, Witticisms & Concise Opinions*, edited by R. Kent Rasmussen; and *Mark Twain: Speaks for Himself*, edited by Paul Fatout, provide a wealth of Twain wit and wisdom that was helpful in writing this book. *Mark Twain A – Z*, by Rasmussen, proved an indispensable reference to Twain's life and times. *The Bible According to Mark Twain*, edited by Howard G. Baetzhold and Joseph B. McCullough is full of mischievous fun, especially regarding the afterlife. Twain's original novels, speeches, and letters—still popular today—are available in many forms at libraries and bookstores. The following books were consulted in the writing of this investment guide.

Ayres, Alex, ed., *The Wit and Wisdom of Mark Twain*. A Meridian Book, 1989.

Baetzhold, Howard G. and McCullough, Joseph B., eds., *The Bible According to Mark Twain*. Touchstone, 1996.

Budd, Louis J., ed. Mark Twain: *Collected Tales, Sketches, Speeches, & Essays 1852–1890*. The Library of America, 1967.

Budd, Louis J., ed. Mark Twain: *Collected Tales, Sketches, Speeches, & Essays 1891–1910*. The Library of America, 1966.

Day, A. Grove, ed., *Mark Twain's Letters from Hawaii*. University of Hawaii Press, 1975.

De Voto, Bernard, ed., *The Portable Mark Twain*. Penguin Books, 1977.

Emerson, Everett, *The Authentic Mark Twain: A Literary Biography of Samuel L. Clemens*. University of Pennsylvania Press, 1984.

Fatout, Paul, ed., *Mark Twain Speaking*. University of Iowa Press, 1976.

Fatout, Paul, ed., *Mark Twain: Speaks for Himself*. Purdue University Press, 1997.

Holms, John P. & Baji, Karin, *Bite-Size Twain: Wit and Wisdom from the Literary Legend*. St. Martin's Press, 1998.

Miller, Robert Keith, *Mark Twain*. Frederick Ungar Publishing Co., Inc., 1983.

Lauber, John, *The Making of Mark Twain*. American Heritage Press, 1985.

Neider, Charles, ed., *The Autobiography of Mark Twain*. HarperPerennial, 1990.

Neider, Charles, ed., *Life as I Find It: A Treasury of Mark Twain Rarities*. Cooper Square Press, 1961.

Neider, Charles, *The Selected Letters of Mark Twain*. Cooper Square Press, 1982.

Quirk, Tom, ed., *Mark Twain: Tales, Speeches, Essays, and Sketches*. Penquin Books, 1994.

Rasmussen, R. Kent, *Mark Twain A – Z*. Oxford University Press, 1995.

Rasmussen, R. Kent, ed., *The Quotable Mark Twain: His Essential Aphorisms, Witticisms & Concise Opinions*. Contemporary Books, 1997.

Twain, Mark, *Adventures of Huckleberry Finn*. University of California Press, 1985.

Twain, Mark, *The Adventures of Tom Sawyer*. University of California Press, 1980.

Twain, Mark, *A Connecticut Yankee in King Arthur's Court*. University of California Press, 1979.

Twain, Mark, *Life on the Mississippi*. Penguin Classics, 1986.

Twain, Mark, *The Mysterious Stranger and Other Stories*. Signet Classic, 1962.

Twain, Mark, *The Prince and the Pauper*. University of California Press, 1993.

Twain, Mark, *Roughing It*. University of California Press, 1993.

Twain, Mark, *Tom Sawyer Abroad: Tom Sawyer Detective*. University of California Press, 1980.

Twain, Mark, *The Unabridged Mark Twain*. Running Press, 1976.

ABOUT THE AUTHOR

Andrew Leckey's financial journalism career includes syndicated newspaper columns, national television reports, and books. He is also a teaching fellow in business journalism at the Graduate School of Journalism of the University of California, Berkeley.

Leckey's "Successful Investing" column is nationally syndicated by the Chicago Tribune Company. He has also been a financial anchor for CNBC cable television network and a reporter for the syndicated "Quicken.com Money Reports" TV spots. He has written a half-dozen books on investment, including *The Morningstar Approach to Investing* (1997) and *Global Investing 2000: A Guide to the 50 Best Stocks in the World* (2000).

The National Association of Investors Corp., which sponsors thousands of investment clubs worldwide, awarded him its "Distinguished Service Award in Investment Education."

Leckey studied business as a Walter Bagehot Fellow at Columbia University, was a fellow of the Media Studies Center in New York City, and respectfully lived in the Mark Twain residence hall while earning his M.A. degree from the University of Missouri School of Journalism.

ABOUT THE CONTRIBUTORS

John C. Bogle, founder and former chairman of The Vanguard Group of mutual funds, is president of its Bogle Financial Market Research Center. An innovator and long-time champion of low-cost, common sense investing, Bogle was named one of the investment industry's four "giants of the 20th century" by *Fortune* magazine. *Bloomberg Personal Finance* magazine designated him one of "12 Minds that Made the Market." Bogle received from alma mater Princeton University the Woodrow Wilson Award for distinguised service in 1999. Books he has written include *Bogle on Mutual Funds* (1993) and *Common Sense on Mutual Funds* (1999).

Louis J. Budd, James B. Duke Professor (Emer.) of English at Duke University, was founding president of the Mark Twain Circle of America and was twice the president of the American Humor Studies Association. He has written *Mark Twain: Social Philosopher* (1962) and *Our Mark Twain: The Making of His Public Personality* (1983). Among several collections about Twain, he has recently edited *Mark Twain: The Contemporary Reviews* (1999).

INDEX